AUGUSTINE DAY BY DAY

AUGUSTINE DAY BY DAY

MINUTE MEDITATIONS FOR EVERY DAY TAKEN FROM THE WRITINGS OF SAINT AUGUSTINE

Compiled and Edited

by

John E. Rotelle, O.S.A.

Illustrated

CATHOLIC BOOK PUBLISHING CO.
New York

CONTENTS

NIHIL OBSTAT: Daniel V. Flynn, J.C.D.
Censor Librorum

IMPRIMATUR: ✠ Joseph T. O'Keefe, D.D
Vicar General, Archdiocese of New York

(T-170)

1 2 3 4 5 6 7 8 9 10 11 12 13 14 15

In Memory of
Father Robert P. Russell, O.S.A.,
who first instilled in me a love for Augustine
and
a desire to know him better,
and
in memory of
Mr. Howard G. Cavalero,
who urged me and guided my efforts
to make Augustine known and appreciated.
An Everlasting Tribute.

PRAYER TO THE HOLY SPIRIT

Breathe into me, Holy Spirit,
    that my thoughts may all be holy.
Move in me, Holy Spirit,
    that my work, too, may be holy.
Attract my heart, Holy Spirit,
    that I may love only what is holy.
Strengthen me, Holy Spirit,
    that I may defend all that is holy.
Protect me, Holy Spirit,
    that I always may be holy.

Attributed to Saint Augustine

PREFACE

ABOUT five years ago I conceived this brilliant idea of preparing a little book of quotes from Saint Augustine for each day of the year. Saint Augustine has much to say to modern society, so I think that pertinent quotes from his writings—especially from his sermons to the people, in which he is so practical and insightful—would benefit many people and help them grow in the way of the Lord.

Over a period of time I gathered these quotes and assigned them to various days of the year, keeping in mind the liturgical seasons.

I completed the manuscript and was putting the finishing touches to it when a confrere of mine, Father John E. Bresnahan, O.S.A., librarian of Augustinian College, Washington, DC, who knew my interest in Augustine, gave me two little books, thinking that I might be interested in them. He did not know at that time of my project of quotes of Augustine for each day of the year.

The books were entitled *Annus Mystico-Augustinianus* by N. Petrelli, O.S.A., published in 1932. The author, with different selections, did exactly what I had contemplated—a calendar of passages from Augustine for each day of the year. A couple of months later the same Father Bresnahan brought to my attention another book in two volumes of passages from Augustine for each day, *Divus Augustinus* by Felice Mayr, O.S.A., published in 1895.

This convinced me that what my father used to say to me was true: "There is nothing new under the sun." Everything is recycled or repackaged.

Both of these publications are different from my own. Not only are the quotes different, but also the basic thrust in both is diverse and the passages are much longer. Perhaps because of the times in which they wrote, the authors emphasize passages that deal with human sinfulness.

What I am trying to do is to present maxims or thoughts from Augustine that apply to present-day situations. Each thought is followed by a prayer. For each day of the year there is a different passage; there are no repetitions. The prayers, however, are repeated from time to time. Since this book is practical in nature, I took the liberty of omitting incidental phrases from the quotes to make the thoughts coherent.

It is my hope that this selection of quotes will encourage people to read Augustine daily, appreciate the timeliness of his thought, experience his perennial youth, and grow from the wisdom of this great man of God. The quotes are brief; the prayers are to the point. Just a few moments of thought each day will lead to immeasurable spiritual benefit for the reader.

The compilation of this book was a work of love for me and convinced me more and more of the beauty and wisdom of Augustine's thought. May all who read it experience the same.

I thank all those who have helped me in any way with this book.

JANUARY 1

Weakness Becomes Strong

HE lies in the manger, but contains the world; He nurses at the breasts, but feeds the angels; He is wrapped in swaddling clothes, but vests us with immortality; He found no place in the inn, but makes for Himself a temple in the hearts of believers.

In order that weakness might become strong, strength became weak. — *Sermon 190, 4*

PRAYER. *My faith prays to You, Lord, the faith You gave me, and inspired in me by the Incarnation of Your Son and the mission of Your preacher.* — *Confessions 1, 1*

JANUARY 2

The Church of Faith

MARY gave birth to your head and the Church gave birth to you.

The Church too is a mother and a virgin-mother because she is made of love, virgin because of the integrity of her faith.

— *Sermon 192, 2*

PRAYER. *May I seek You, Lord, by praying to You, and let me pray to You by believing in You.*

— *Confessions 1, 1*

JANUARY 3

The Humble Person

WHY does a person always praise the Lord? Because that person is humble. What does it mean to be humble? It means to be unwilling to be praised in oneself.

Those who wish to be praised in themselves are proud. Those who are not proud are humble.

— *Commentary on Psalm 33 (2), 5*

PRAYER. *Lord, how exalted You are and yet the humble of heart are Your dwelling.*

— *Confessions 11, 31*

JANUARY 4

Whoever Comes to Me Becomes Humble

I CAME in humility, I came to teach humility, I came as a model of humility. Whoever comes to Me is incorporated in Me.

Whoever comes to Me becomes humble; whoever adheres to My will will be humble, for such a person does not perform his or her own will, but the will of God. And therefore he or she will not be cast out. — *Sermon on John 25, 16*

PRAYER. *Lord, You exist without care for Your own security, but are full of concern for us.*

— *Confessions 9, 3*

JANUARY 5

The Virgin Mary

 THE virgin Mother gave birth from her fruitful womb and inviolate body to Him Who became visible for us, to Him by Whom while He was invisible she had been created.

While conceiving, she was a virgin, while giving birth she was a virgin, a virgin in her pregnancy, a virgin while carrying her son, a virgin forever. — *Sermon 186, 1*

PRAYER. *O Lord God, give us Your Christ, let us know Your Christ, let us see Your Christ, not as the Jews saw Him, and then crucified him, but as the angels see Him and rejoice.*

— *Commentary on Psalm, 84, 9*

JANUARY 6

A Man in Time

 E so loved us that, for our sake, He was made man in time, although through Him all times were made. He was made man, Who made man.

He was created of a mother whom He created. He was carried by hands that He formed. He cried in the manger in wordless infancy, He the Word, without Whom all human eloquence is mute. — *Sermon 188, 2*

PRAYER. *I realize what I am and praise You for it. Come to my aid, that I may not stray from the way of salvation.* — *Sermon 67, 9*

JANUARY 7

The Source of Light

BVIOUSLY, if you could be enlightened by yourself, you would never be in the dark, because you are always with yourself.

Do not believe that you are a light to yourself. The Light is that which illumines every person coming into this world.

— *Commentary on Psalm 25 (2), 11*

PRAYER. *Happiness is joy in the truth because it is joy in You, O Lord, Who are truth, my light, my salvation, my God.* — *Confessions 10, 23*

JANUARY 8

Without Humility Pride Will Win

RASP the truth of God by using the way He Himself provides, since He sees the weakness of our footsteps. That way consists first, of humility, second, of humility, and third, of humility.

Unless humility precede, accompany, and follow up all the good we accomplish, unless we keep our eyes fixed on it, pride will snatch everything right out of our hands. — *Letter 118, 22*

PRAYER. *I acknowledge You, O Lord, in Your humility, that I may not fear You in Your glory. I embrace You in Your lowliness, that I may yearn for You in Your loftiness, for to those who desire You, You come with clemency.*

— *Psalm 66, 10*

JANUARY 9

The Root of Friendship

YOU did not look down on being the friend of the humble and returning the love that was shown to you.

For what else is friendship but this? It gets its name from love alone, is faithful only in Christ, and in Him alone can it be eternal and happy.
— *Against Two Pelagian Letters 1, 1*

PRAYER. *Lord, heal and open my eyes that I may recognize Your will. Show me the road I must travel that I may see You.* — *Soliloquies 1, 5*

JANUARY 10

Men and Women Aching for God

EVERYTHING could well have been done by an angel, but the standing of the human race would have been devalued if God had seemed unwilling to let humans act as agents of His word to others.

On top of that, charity itself, which binds people together in the tight knot of unity, would have no means of expressing itself, by pouring out, and as it were mixing together the souls of humans, if human beings could learn nothing from others.
— *Christian Doctrine, Preface 6*

PRAYER. *I call upon You, my God, my mercy, my creator. I had forgotten You, but you held me ever in Your sight.* — *Confessions 13, 1*

JANUARY 11

The Hymn of Love

LOVE that strains after the possession of the loved object is desire; and the love that possesses and enjoys that object is joy. The love that shuns what opposes it is fear, while the love that feels that opposition when it happens is grief.

Consequently, these feelings are bad, if the love is bad, and good if the love is good.

— *City of God 14, 7*

PRAYER. *O Lord, I love You. I love, I burn, I pant for You; I trample under foot all that gives here delight. I want to go to You.* — *Sermon 159, 8*

JANUARY 12

Change People, and Times Will Be Changed

YOU say, the times are troublesome, the times are burdensome, the times are miserable. Live rightly and you will change the times.

The times have never hurt anyone. Those who are hurt are human beings; those by whom they are hurt are also human beings. So, change human beings and the times will be changed.

— *Sermon 311, 8*

PRAYER. *Let my soul rouse itself, Lord, from weariness, lean on Your creation and hobble toward You Who made it all. For in You we are remade and find true strength.* — *Confessions 5, 1*

14

JANUARY 13

Conceive Christ by Faith

IN Mary holy virginity gave birth to Christ; in Anna, aged widowhood recognized Christ in the child; in Elizabeth, conjugal chastity did service for Christ. All ranks of the faithful have contributed to the Head according to their ability.

Therefore, since Christ is Truth and Peace and Justice, conceive Him by faith, bring Him forth by works, so that what the womb of Mary did in the flesh of Christ your heart may do in the law of Christ. — *Sermon 192, 2*

PRAYER. *Father, a closed heart cannot keep out Your gaze. You open it as You please in mercy or in justice. Nothing can hide from Your heat.*
— *Confessions 5, 1*

JANUARY 14

Dreams and Reality

A BEGGAR, lying on the bare ground and trembling from cold, falls asleep and dreams of treasures; in his dream he rejoices and grows arrogant, and will not even spare a glance for his own father who is clothed in rags.

As long as he has not awakened he is rich; but the greater the empty joy he experiences in sleep, the more, when he awakens, will he suffer from reality. — *Sermon 345, 1*

PRAYER. *O happy home! O land of safety! May I dwell there in security!* — *Sermon 217, 2*

JANUARY 15

Be Like the Deer

CHARITY makes us support one another in bearing our burdens. When the deer have to cross a river, each one of them carries on its back the head of the one following while it rests its head on the back of the one preceding.

In that way, supporting and helping each other, they are able to cross safely wide rivers, until they reach together the stability of the land.

— *Eighty-three Diverse Questions, 71, 1*

PRAYER. *O Lord, my God, pay heed to my prayer. Look with mercy on my desire, which is not concerned with myself alone, but with my neighbor's good as well.* — *Confessions 11, 2*

JANUARY 16

Observe the Local Custom

WHEN my mother reached Milan, she found the church there not fasting on Saturdays. She was troubled, and hesitated as to what she should do.

I applied on her behalf to Ambrose for his advice. He replied, "When I go to Rome, I also fast on Saturday: when here, I do not. If you go to any church, observe the local custom."

— *Letter 54, 2*

PRAYER. *Lord, while I was still far away from You, You coaxed me in a great many ways to hear You from afar and be converted to You and call upon You.* — *Confessions 13, 1*

JANUARY 17

Possess What You Need

Y brothers and sisters, seek what is enough for God's work, not what is sufficient for your greediness. Your greediness is no work of God.

Your self, your body, your soul, this is all God's work. Inquire what is enough for them, and you shall see how little it is.

— Commentary on Psalm 147, 12

PRAYER. *Lord, those are Your best servants who wish to shape their life on Your answers rather than shape Your answers on their wishes.*

— Confessions 10, 26

JANUARY 18

Keep on Moving

N earth we are wayfarers, always on the go. This means that we have to keep on moving forward. Therefore be always unhappy about what you are if you want to reach what you are not.

If you are pleased with what you are, you have stopped already. If you say; "It is enough," you are lost. Keep on walking, moving forward, trying for the goal. Don't try to stop on the way, or to go back, or to deviate from it.   *— Sermon 169, 18*

PRAYER. *Lord, guard us from all danger and carry us to Yourself. And You will be our strong support from childhood to old age; for when our strength is Yours, we are strong.*

— Confessions 4, 16

JANUARY 19

The Treasures of Scripture

THE depth of the Christian Scriptures is boundless. Even if I were attempting to study them and nothing else, from boyhood to decrepit old age, with the utmost leisure, the most unwearied zeal, and with talents greater than I possess, I would still be making progress in discovering their treasures

— *Letter 137, 3*

PRAYER. *O Lord my God, let my soul praise You that it may love You. Let it recount to You Your mercies that it may praise You for them all.*

— *Confessions 5, 1*

JANUARY 20

The Grace of God

PREVIOUSLY I had tried hard to uphold the freedom of choice of the human will; but the grace of God had the upper hand.

The Apostle Paul stated the most obvious truth, when he said: "What have you got that you did not first receive? If you have received all this, why glory in it as if you had not been given it?"

— *Revisions 2, 27*

PRAYER. *I thank You, Lord, my joy and my glory, my hope and my God. I thank You for Your gifts to me. Keep them unharmed for me: they will be the making of me, and I shall be with You for my being is Your gift.*

— *Confessions 1, 20*

JANUARY 21

Knowledge by Writings

I T is also necessary—may God grant it!—that in providing others with books to read I myself should make progress, and that in trying to answer their questions I myself should find what I am seeking.

Therefore, at the command of God our Lord and with His help, I have undertaken not so much to discourse with authority on matters known to me as to know them better by discoursing devoutly of them. — *The Trinity 1, 8*

PRAYER. Lord, let me offer You the sacrifice of every thought and word—only first give me what I may offer You. — *Confessions 11, 2*

JANUARY 22

Getting Dressed

E VERY morning you put on your clothes to cover your nakedness and to protect your body from the inclement weather. Why don't you also clothe your soul with the garment of faith?

Remember every morning the truths of your creed, and look at yourself in the mirror of your faith. Otherwise, your soul will soon be naked with the nakedness of oblivion. — *Sermon 58, 13*

PRAYER. Lord, only this do I ask of Your great kindness: that You convert me totally to You and allow no obstacle to hinder me as I wend my way to You. — *Soliloquies 1, 6*

JANUARY 23

Avoid Pride and Grasp Wisdom

AFTER hearing that they should be humble some persons do not wish to learn anything.

They think they will be proud if they have anything. It has been made clear to us where God wishes us to be in the depths and where he wishes us to be in the heights. He wishes us to be humble to avoid pride, and He wishes us to be on high to grasp wisdom.

— Commentary on Psalm 130, 12

PRAYER. *While I move and bear this body I pray that I may be pure, generous, just, and prudent. May I be a perfect lover and knower of Your Wisdom.*
— Soliloquies 1, 6

JANUARY 24

My Weight Is My Love

GRAVITY keeps everything in its own place. Fire climbs up, while a stone goes down. Elements that are not in their own place are restless until they find it.

This applies also to us. My weight is my love; wherever I go, I am driven by it. By the love of God we catch fire ourselves and, by moving up, find our place and our rest. *— Confessions 13, 9*

PRAYER. *Come, Lord, into my soul, which You have prepared for Your own reception by inspiring in me a longing for Your goodness.*
— Confessions 13, 1

JANUARY 25
The Faith of Abraham

LET us every day do our best to advance in God, and to be unsparing with the transitory possessions we are going to leave behind us in this world. Let us pay attention to Abraham's faith, because he was also our father. Let us imitate his devotion and faith.

We are Christians, and strangers on earth. Let none of us be frightened; our native land is not in this world. — *Sermon 16A, 13*

PRAYER. God examines both rich and poor, not according to their lands and houses, but according to the riches of their hearts.

— *Commentary on Psalm 48 (1), 3*

JANUARY 26
Renewed by Love

PEOPLE are renewed by love. As sinful desire ages them, so love rejuvenates them. Enmeshed in the toils of his desires the psalmist laments: "I have grown old surrounded by my enemies."

Love, on the other hand, is the sign of our renewal as we know from the Lord's own words: "I give you a new commandment—love one another." — *Sermon 350A, 21*

PRAYER. Lord, those who are bowed down with burdens You lift up, and they do not fall because You are their support. — *Confessions 11, 31*

JANUARY 27

The Sensitive Person

IVE me persons in love: they know what I mean. Give me those who yearn; give me those who are hungry; give me those far away in this desert, who are thirsty and sigh for the spring of the eternal country. Give me those kinds of people: they know what I mean.

But if I speak to cold persons, they just do not know what I am talking about.

— Sermon on John 26. 4

PRAYER. *Instruct me, Lord, and command what You will. But first heal me and open my ears that I may hear Your words.* *— Soliloquies 1, 5*

JANUARY 28

Prayer from the Heart

HE pure prayer that ascends from a faithful heart will be like incense rising from a hallowed altar.

No fragrance can be more pleasing to God than that of His own Son. May all the faithful breathe out the same perfume.

— Commentary on Psalm 140, 6

PRAYER. *Lord, I am poor and needy, and You are generous to all who appeal to You.*

— Confessions 11, 2

JANUARY 29
Love God's Creation

SUPPOSE a man should make a ring for his betrothed, and she should love the ring more wholeheartedly than the betrothed who made it for her. Certainly, let her love his gift: but if she should say, "The ring is enough. I do not want to see his face again," what would we say of her?

The pledge is given her by the betrothed just that, in his pledge, he himself may be loved. God, then has given you all these things. Love Him Who made them. — *Sermon on 1 John 2, 11*

PRAYER. *Lord, let those who understand, praise You, and let those who understand You not, praise You too.* — *Confessions 11, 31*

JANUARY 30
Putting Up with All That Is Annoying

NOW, what does "Let him take up his cross mean"? Put up with all that is annoying: that is how they must follow Me. To tell the truth, when they follow Me, imitating My conduct and keeping My commandments, they will have many who will try to oppose them, forbid them, dissuade them, and this will be done by those same people who appear to be followers of Christ. — *Sermon 96, 4.*

PRAYER. *O Lord my God, what is the kernel of Your deep mystery? How far from it have I been led by the consequences of my sins!*

— *Confessions 11, 31*

JANUARY 31

The Meaning of Good People

WHEN we are weighed down by poverty, and grief makes us sad; when bodily pain makes us restless, and exile despondent; or when any other grievance afflicts us, if there be good people at hand who understand the art of rejoicing with the joyful and weeping with the sorrowful, who know how to speak a cheerful word and uplift us, then bitterness is mitigated, worries are alleviated, and our troubles are overcome.

— Letter 130, 2.

PRAYER. *Lord, whether prosperity smile or adversity frown, let Your praise be ever in my mouth.* — *Commentary on Psalm 138, 16*

FEBRUARY 1

Call Upon the Lord

YOU have made us for Yourself, O Lord, and our hearts are restless until they rest in You. Grant me, O Lord to know and understand which comes first: to call upon You or to praise You; and whether first to know You or call upon You.

How are they to call upon Him in Whom they have not believed? How are they to believe in Him Whom they have not heard? And they who seek the Lord shall praise Him. — *Confessions 1, 1*

PRAYER. *May I seek You, Lord, by praying to You, and let me pray to You by believing in You.*

— Confessions 1, 1

FEBRUARY 2

The Christ of the Temple

CHRIST is born in a humble inn, wrapped in swaddling clothes, and laid in a manger. Then the Lord of heaven and earth, the creator of angels, the author and maker of all things visible and invisible, suckles, cries, is nourished, grows, endures His age, and hides His majesty.

Afterward He is bound, despised, scourged, jeered, spat at, struck, crowned with thorns, hung on a cross, and pierced with a spear. What poverty is there! — *Sermon 14, 9*

PRAYER. *Lord, I am poor and needy. I am better only when with heartfelt sorrow I renounce myself and seek Your mercy so that my deficiencies are overcome and transformed.* — *Confessions 10, 38*

FEBRUARY 3

Be within the Law

IT is one thing to be within the law and another thing to be under the law. Those who are within the law act according to the law. Those who are under the law are acted upon according to the law.

Therefore, those who are within the law are free; those who are under the law are slaves.

— *Commentary on Psalm 1, 2*

PRAYER. *O God, You are the Truth and the Light of my heart. Let me listen to You and not to the darkness within me.* — *Confessions 12, 10*

FEBRUARY 4
Don't Turn Your Back on God

ET no one say: "I am leaving the monastery because monks are not the only ones who can reach the kingdom of God; those outside the monastery also belong to God."

Those outside the monastery certainly belong to God; but they have not taken vows (common life and continence). You, however, have taken them, and now you are going back on them.

— *Commentary on Psalm 75, 16*

PRAYER. *Keep your eyes fixed on the Lord, Who guides you, and do not look back.*

— *Commentary on Psalm 75, 16*

FEBRUARY 5
Living Together and Marriage

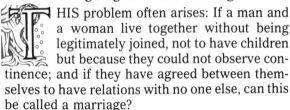HIS problem often arises: If a man and a woman live together without being legitimately joined, not to have children but because they could not observe continence; and if they have agreed between themselves to have relations with no one else, can this be called a marriage?

Perhaps, but only if they have resolved to maintain until death the good faith that they had promised to themselves, even though this union did not rest on a desire to have children.

— *The Good of Marriage, 5, 5*

PRAYER. *Lord, You change Your works, but Your design is always the same.* — *Confessions 1, 4*

FEBRUARY 6

The Delight of Friendship

ALL kinds of things rejoiced my soul in their company—to talk and laugh, and to do other kindnesses; to read pleasant books together; to pass from lightest jesting to talk of the deepest things and back again; to differ without rancor, as persons might differ with themselves, and when most rarely dissension arose, to find our normal agreement all the sweeter for it; to teach each other and to learn from each other.

These and such things kindled a flame that fused our very souls together and made us one out of many. — *Confessions 4, 8*

PRAYER. *Blessed are those who love You, O Lord, and love their friends in You and their enemies because of You.* — *Confessions 4, 9*

FEBRUARY 7

Praising God

YOU are praising God when you do your day's work. You are praising Him when you eat and drink. You are praising Him when you rest on your bed. You are praising Him when you are asleep.

So when are you not praising Him?

— *Commentary on Psalm 146, 2*

PRAYER. *Human beings are Your creatures, Lord, and their instinct is to praise You.*

— *Confessions 1, 1*

FEBRUARY 8

Good Pupils

CHRISTIANS must seek to advance toward God every day and always to rejoice in God or in His gifts. Our exile here on earth is very short, and our native land is timeless. Here we seek devotion to God, but there we rest.

We must calculate our gains daily. We must be not only eager listeners but careful workers. This school of life, in which God is the only teacher, looks for good pupils who will not desert but remain loyal. — *Sermon 16A, 1*

PRAYER. *May God in His mercy grant that every day we may be troubled, tried, disciplined, or make some progress.* — *Sermon 16A, 12*

FEBRUARY 9

Abstain and Sustain

TWO are the commands given us for this life of ours; to abstain and to sustain. To abstain from those things that are considered good by the world, and to sustain the many things that are bad in the world.

This requires continence and endurance. Continence means not to rely on worldly happiness. Endurance signifies not to give way to worldly unhappiness. — *Sermon 38, 1*

PRAYER. *Lord, You are with us. You deliver us from our wretched errors, establish us on Your path, and encourage us.* — *Confessions 6, 16*

FEBRUARY 10

The Marks of Good Superiors

OOD superiors rebuke those who stir up strife, comfort those of little courage, take the part of the weak, refute opponents, and guard against traps.

They teach the ignorant, awake the indolent, put the presumptuous in their place, mollify the quarrelsome, help the poor, liberate the oppressed, encourage the good, suffer the wicked, and love everyone. — *Sermon 140, 1*

PRAYER. *Lord, You love us with a love that is true.* — *Confessions 1, 4*

FEBRUARY 11

Take Account of Failures

AS long as we are human beings, we cannot avoid failures, even if they are flimsy. What is important in any case is not to ignore them, not to disregard them. For swollen rivers are made out of small drops of water.

A tiny leak in a boat, unless noticed and controlled in time, is cause enough for the boat to sink to the bottom of the sea. Drop by drop the hull will be flooded, and the boat will get heavier until finally it cannot float anymore.

— *Sermon 58, 9-10*

PRAYER. *Lord, You grieve over wrongdoing, but You feel no pain.* — *Confessions 1, 4*

FEBRUARY 12

The Force of Habit

ORD, sometimes You fill me with a feeling quite unlike my normal state. This gives me an inward sense of delight, which if it were to reach fulfillment in me would be something entirely different from my present life.

But my heavy burden of distress drags me back. I am sucked back to my habits and find myself held fast; I weep greatly, but I am firmly held. The load of habit is a force to be reckoned with! — *Confessions 10, 40*

PRAYER. You have accompanied me on my path, O Truth, teaching me what to avoid and what to desire. — *Confessions 10, 40*

FEBRUARY 13

A Cheap Old Song

OU are thinking that I am saying what I always say; and you go on doing what you always do. What shall I do—now that I seem just a cheap old song to you? Change, change, I beseech you.

The end of life is always unpredictable. Each of us walks with a chance of falling. I beseech you, brothers and sisters, even if you have forgotten about yourselves, at least take some pity on me.

— *Sermon 232, 8*

PRAYER. Lord, You support, fill, and over-shadow all things. — *Confessions 1, 4*

FEBRUARY 14

The Inner Teacher

THERE is a Master within Who teaches us. Christ is our Master, and His inspiration teaches us. Where His inspiration and His unction are lacking, it is in vain that words resound in our ears. As Paul the Apostle said: "I planted the seed and Apollos watered it, but God made it grow."

Therefore, whether we plant or whether we water by our words, we are nothing. It is God Who gives the increase; His unction teaches you all things.
— *Sermon on 1 John 3, 13*

PRAYER. *You, Lord, are the unfailing light, and from You I sought to know the existence, nature, and worth of all things, as I listened to Your teaching and commandments.*

— *Confessions 10, 40*

FEBRUARY 15

The Lesson of Ashes

WILL these ashes one day take on the form of beauty, be restored to life, restored to light? The bodies of all of us will in a few years be ashes. Yet a few years ago we were not even ashes!

If God was able to create what did not exist, will He not be able to remake what once existed?
— *Sermon 361, 12*

PRAYER. *Lord, You are never new and never old. Yet You give new life to all things.*

— *Confessions 1, 4*

FEBRUARY 16

God's Mercy Is Our Hope

RIVEN out of paradise by You and exiled in a distant land, I cannot return by myself unless You, O Lord, come to meet me in my wandering. My return is based on hope in Your mercy during all of my earthly life.

My only hope, the only source of confidence, and the only solid promise is Your mercy.

— *Commentary on Psalm 24, 5*

PRAYER. *My God, let me remember You with thanksgiving and proclaim Your mercies to me.*

— *Confessions 8, 1*

FEBRUARY 17

You Approached Me

ETERNAL Truth and true Love and beloved Eternity: You are my God, and for You do I sigh night and day. When I first began to know You, You lifted me up that I might see that there was something to be seen—but I was as yet not able to see it.

Then You drove back the weakness of my sight, shining upon me most powerfully, and I shook with love and fear. — *Confessions 7, 10*

PRAYER. *Lord, You first sought me out and brought me back on Your shoulder.*

— *Commentary on Psalm 69, 6*

FEBRUARY 18

The Inner Light

I ENTERED into my inmost self with You, Lord, as my guide; and this I was able to do because You were my helper. I entered in and saw with the eye of my soul, the unchangeable Light, very different from earthly lights.

It was above my mind but not the way oil is above water or heaven above the earth. It was superior because it made me, and I inferior because I was made by it. Those who know the truth know this light, and those who know it know eternity: it is charity that knows it.

— *Confessions 7, 10*

PRAYER. *Lord, You are the light of my heart and the bread in the mouth of my soul.*

— *Confessions 1, 13*

FEBRUARY 19

Maintaining Sound Doctrine

SOUND doctrine must be maintained. We must never judge in arrogant haughtiness persons who do not embrace our mode of life.

We must never say that it is no use for them to live chastely in the married state, to direct their houses and families in a Christian way, or to heap up for themselves heavenly treasures by their acts of mercy. — *Letter 157, 39*

PRAYER. *Lord, You get angry but remain calm.*

— *Confessions 1, 4*

FEBRUARY 20
Hold Fast to the Love of God

REAL love of God will not be in you if the love of the world prevails in you. Hold fast rather to the love of God, so that as God is eternal you too will live forever. For each of us is such as our love is.

Do you love the world? Then you will be the earth. Do you love God? What shall I say? That you will be a god? I dare not say this on my own authority, and so let us hear Holy Scripture: "I have said: you are gods and all of you children of the Most High." — *Sermon on John 2, 8*

PRAYER. *Lord, teach me what I should teach, teach me what I should hold fast.* — *Letter 166, 10*

FEBRUARY 21
Let the Better Love Take Over

THERE are two loves, the love of God and the love of the world. If the love of the world takes possession of you, there is no way for the love of God to enter into you.

Let the love of the world take the second place, and let the love of God dwell in you. Let the better love take over. — *Sermon on 1 John 2, 8*

PRAYER. *O to love! to go and be lost to self! to reach God!* — *Sermon 159, 8*

FEBRUARY 22
True Priestly Service

LEARLY, there is nothing easier, more pleasureful, or more sought after than the office of bishop, priest, or deacon if this is going to be carried out lightly, amid the blandishments of flatterers. But in the eyes of God, there is nothing more miserable, more regrettable, or more worthy of condemnation.

On the other hand, provided this service is carried out as our Master commands, in the eyes of God there is no greater happiness. — *Letter 21, 1*

PRAYER. *Lord, You are never needy, yet You are pleased with gain. You are never covetous, yet You exact interest on all You give us.*

— *Confessions 1, 4*

FEBRUARY 23
The Value of Mortification

HAT else is that cross of ours which the Lord commands us to carry if not the mortality of our flesh? It is a source of distress to us until death is swallowed up in victory.

Therefore, it is precisely this cross that we must crucify and pierce with the nails of the fear of God. — *Letter 243, 11*

PRAYER. *Are there any persons, Lord, who do not at times let themselves go beyond the strict limits of necessity? I am not one of them, for I am a sinner.* — *Confessions 10, 31*

FEBRUARY 24

Excess in Eating and Drinking

I STRUGGLE each day against concupiscence in eating and drinking. It is not something that I can resolve to cut off once and for all and touch no more, as I could with concubinage. The bridle put upon the throat must be held with moderate looseness and moderate firmness.

Is there anyone, Lord, who is not carried a little beyond the limits of personal need?

— *Confessions 10, 31*

PRAYER. *O holy God, it is You Who give us the power to do what You command.*

— *Confessions 10, 31*

FEBRUARY 25

Temptations out of the Past

LORD, You command me to be continent. You have commanded me to abstain from concubinage, and in place of marriage itself—which You permit—You have counseled something better.

Since You granted this to me, it has been fulfilled even before I became a dispenser of Your sacrament. Yet, in my memory, of which I have said many things, there still live images of such things as my former habits implanted there.

— *Confessions 10, 30*

PRAYER. *Your hand, O God Almighty, is able to heal all the infirmities of my soul.*

— *Confessions 10, 30*

FEBRUARY 26
True Fasting

YOUR fast would be rejected if you were immoderately severe toward your servant. Will it be approved if you fail to recognize your brother or sister?

I am not asking what food you abstain from, but what you love. Do you love justice? Well, then, let your justice be seen.

— *The Value of Fasting 5, 6-7*

PRAYER. *O Lord, You will increase Your gifts more and more in me, so that set free from all concupiscence my soul may follow me to You.*

— *Confessions 10, 30*

FEBRUARY 27
Everything Works Together for Charity

ALL these endeavors for fasting are concerned not about the rejection of various foods as unclean, but about the subjugation of inordinate desire and the maintenance of neighborly love.

Charity especially is guarded: food is subservient to charity, speech to charity, customs to charity, and facial expressions to charity. Everything works together for charity alone.

— *Customs of the Catholic Church, 33, 70*

PRAYER. *How great was Your love for us, kind Father! You did not spare Your only-begotten Son but surrendered Him for the sake of us sinners!* — *Confessions 10, 43*

FEBRUARY 28

Pride—the Beginning of All Sin

O other cause but pride could have been the beginning of our first parents' evil will? For pride is the beginning of all sin. What is pride but the desire of a height out of proportion to our state?

Furthermore, it is a height out of proportion to our state to leave God—to whom the soul should cling as its basis—and to become and to be in some way our own basis. *— City of God 14, 13*

PRAYER. *You, Lord, are the unseen power that brings decline upon the proud.* *— Confessions 1, 4*

MARCH 1

The Promised Gift

HRIST grants justification to those who believe in Him, simply because they have faith and not because they observe the law. The blessing granted to Abraham for his exemplary faith is extended to the Gentiles, so that we may receive the promised Spirit through faith.

In other words, the promised gift to believers is not a spirit of outward observance but one of inward devotion inspired by love.

— Commentary on Galatians 22

PRAYER. *O truly full of grace! Who can explain this grace? Who is able to give thanks for this grace?* *— Sermon 290, 5*

MARCH 2
Life Entails Change

RIGHT reason demands a change in what was right to do at some earlier time if the time or circumstance is changed.

Therefore, when objectors say it is not right to make a change, truth answers with a shout that it is not right not to make a change.

— Letter 138

PRAYER. *Lord, You are always preparing things. You prepare us for Yourself, and Yourself for us. You prepare a place for Yourself in us, and for us in Yourself.* — *Sermon on John 68, 3*

MARCH 3

Bear One Another's Burdens

THE responsibility of love is that we bear one another's burdens. But this responsibility, which is not an eternal one, leads doubtless to an eternal blessedness in which there will be no burdens for us that we will be required to bear for one another.

Now, however, while we are in this life, that is, on this journey, let us bear one another's burdens so that we can achieve that life which is free of every burden.

— Eighty-three Diverse Questions, 71

PRAYER. *Lord, inspire me with love, that I may teach sweetness. Give me patience, that I may teach discipline. Enlighten my understanding, that I teach wisdom.*

— Commentary on Psalm 118 (17), 4

MARCH 4

Causes of Punishment

YOU who boast of the punishment you endure, do you fail to see that there were three crosses when our Lord suffered? The Lord suffered between two thieves.

It was not the punishment that distinguished them, but the cause for which they were punished. — *Sermon 325, 2*

PRAYER. *You are one God, and You come to my aid. In You nothing is lacking and nothing is in excess. In You the one who generates and the one generated are one alone.* — *Soliloquies 1, 4*

MARCH 5

Our All-powerful Physician

OUR wound is serious, but the Physician is all-powerful. Does it seem to you so small a mercy that, while you were living in evil and sinning, He did not take away your life, but brought you to belief and forgave your sins?

What I suffer is serious, but I trust the Almighty. I would despair of my mortal wound if I had not found so great a Physician.

— *Sermon 352, 3*

PRAYER. *Bring relief to a serious wound with Your great medicine. Mine is serious, but I take refuge in the Almighty.*
— *Commentary on Psalm 50, 6*

MARCH 6

Jesus Overcame the Curse

JESUS overcame the curse on the human race by taking it upon His own person. He vanquished death by undergoing death Himself, sin by identifying Himself with sin, and the ancient serpent by another serpent.

Death, sin, and the serpent were all included in God's curse on the human race after the first sin, but the cross has triumphed over each of them.

— *Commentary on Galatians 22*

PRAYER. You are the truest Lord. You are not like lords who buy with their wallets, but the Lord Who buys with blood. You give me the strength of salvation.

— *Commentary on Psalm 139, 11*

MARCH 7

We Pray to Him, through Him, and in Him

WE pray to Christ as God, and He prays for us as a servant. In the first case he is the Creator, in the second a creature. Himself unchanged, He took to Himself our created nature in order to change it, and He made us one man with Himself, Head and Body.

We pray then to Him, through Him, and in Him. We speak along with Him, and He speaks along with us. — *Commentary on Psalm 85, 1*

PRAYER. I pray to You, God, for You lead us to every truth, tell us of every good thing, and let us come to no harm. — *Soliloquies 1, 3*

MARCH 8

Daily Progress toward God

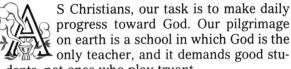

AS Christians, our task is to make daily progress toward God. Our pilgrimage on earth is a school in which God is the only teacher, and it demands good students, not ones who play truant.

In this school we learn something every day. We learn something from commandments, something from examples, and something from Sacraments. These things are remedies for our wounds and materials for our studies.   — *Sermon 16A, 1*

PRAYER.   *Lord, You help those who turn to You. You redeem us so that we may come to You.*

— *Commentary on Psalm 17, 15*

MARCH 9

God Calls Us to Conversion

GOD calls us to correct ourselves and invites us to do penance. He calls us through the wonderful gifts of His creation, and He calls us by granting time for life.

He calls us through the reader and through the preacher. He calls us with the innermost force of our thoughts. He calls us with the scourge of punishment, and He calls us with the mercy of His consolation.   — *Commentary on Psalm 102, 16*

PRAYER.   *Lord, see Your work in me, not my own. For if You see my own work, You condemn me; but if You see Yours, You crown me.*

— *Commentary on Psalm 137, 18*

MARCH 10

Tomorrow May Never Come

GOD is not now so long-suffering in putting up with you that He will fail to be just in punishing. Do not say then: "Tomorrow I shall be converted, tomorrow I shall please God, and all that I shall have done today and yesterday will be forgiven me."

What you say is true: God has promised forgiveness if you turn back to Him. But what He has not promised is that you will have tomorrow in which to achieve your conversion.

— *Commentary on Psalm 144, 11*

PRAYER. *Come, Lord, and act. Rouse and renew us; kindle us and carry us away; shine before us and be gentle with us. Let us love and run toward You.* — *Confessions 8, 4*

MARCH 11

The Lord Turns Us toward Him

LORD, You help us as we move toward You. Grant that we may never attribute to our own wisdom the fact that we are converted to You. Neither let us ever attribute to our strength the fact that we actually reach You.

In this way we will avoid being repelled by You Who resist the proud.

— *Commentary on Psalm 18 (1), 15*

PRAYER. *Lord, help us, so that a change may be achieved in us and we find You ready to offer Yourself for the enjoyment of those who love You.* — *Commentary on Psalm 6, 5*

MARCH 12

The Gift of Being Good

E Who has given us the gift of being gives us also the gift of being good. He gives to those who have turned back to Him. He even sought them out before they were converted and when they were far from His ways! — *Commentary on Psalm 103 (4), 2*

PRAYER. *Lord, command and requisition whatever You wish. But heal and open my ears so that I may hear Your voice. Heal and open my eyes so that I may see You commanding. Drive the madness out of me so that I may recognize You.* — *Soliloquies 1, 5*

MARCH 13

The Mercy of the Shepherd

LTHOUGH the lost sheep could lose itself while wandering, it could not find itself. It would not have been found if the mercy of the shepherd had not sought it out.

Similarly, the prodigal son was also sought out and raised up by the One Who gives life to all things. And by whom was he found if not by the One Who came to save and seek out what was lost? — *Commentary on Psalm 77, 24*

PRAYER. *Lord, I have done much wrong and I cannot hope for a speedy rest for myself; may my torments be enough till Your coming. Let me be tortured now; then, when You come, spare me.*

— *Sermon 327, 2*

MARCH 14

Lent—the Epitome of Our Whole Life

CHRISTIANS must always live in this way, without any wish to come down from their cross—otherwise they will sink beneath the world's mire. But if we have to do so all our lives, we must make an even greater effort during the days of Lent.

It is not a simple matter of living through forty days. Lent is the epitome of our whole life.

— *Sermon 205, 1*

PRAYER. *Lord Jesus, You suffered for us not for Yourself. You bore the punishment for no fault of Your own so that You might abolish both the fault and the punishment.* — *Sermon 136, 6*

MARCH 15

Daily Remedy for Sin

FORGIVE us our debts as we also forgive our debtors. Let us say this sentence with sincerity, because it is an alms in itself. Sins that oppress and bury us cannot be termed trifles! What is more minute than drops of rain? Yet they fill the rivers. What is more minute than grains of wheat? Yet they fill the barns.

You note the fact that these sins are rather small, but You do not take note that there are many of them. In any case, God has given us a daily remedy for them. — *Sermon 261, 10*

PRAYER. *"Our Father in heaven, forgive us our debts as we forgive our debtors."*

— *Sermon 261, 10*

MARCH 16

Perseverance in the Midst of Trials

YOUR first task is to be dissatisfied with yourself, fight sin, and transform yourself into something better.

Your second task is to put up with the trials and temptations of this world that will be brought on by the change in your life and to persevere to the very end in the midst of these things. — *Commentary on Psalm 59, 5*

PRAYER. Lord, our God, we hope in the shelter of Your wings. Protect and carry us. It is only when You are our strength that we are strong.

— *Confessions 4, 16*

MARCH 17

Granting Pardon

PARDON, that you may be pardoned. In doing this, nothing is required of the body. It is the will that acts. You will experience no physical pain; you will have nothing less in your home.

Now in truth, my brothers and sisters, you see what an evil it is that those who have been commanded to love even their enemy do not pardon a penitent brother or sister. — *Sermon 210, 10*

PRAYER. I pray You, my God, Who are Truth, I pray You to forgive my sins. — *Confessions 11, 3*

MARCH 18

Asking Forgiveness of Others

OW many there are who know that they have sinned against their brothers or sisters and yet are unwilling to say: "Forgive me."

They were not ashamed to sin, but they are ashamed to ask pardon. They were not ashamed of their evil act, but they blush where humility is concerned. — *Sermon 211, 4*

PRAYER. *I implore You, my God, to Whom faith calls us, hope leads us, and love unites us: come to me in Your mercy.* — *Soliloquies 1, 3*

MARCH 19

It Is God Who Initiates Conversion

ID you make it possible for yourselves to merit God's mercy because you turned back to him? If you hadn't been called by God, what could you have done to turn back? Didn't the very One Who called you when you were opposed to Him make it possible for you to turn back?

Don't claim your conversion as your own doing. Unless He had called you when you were running away from Him, you would not have been able to turn back.

— *Commentary on Psalm 84, 8*

PRAYER. *Let me not be my own life. I have lived badly on my own account and been death to myself, but in You I live again. Speak to me, O Lord.*

— *Confessions 12, 10*

MARCH 20

Help for a Complete Conversion

WHEN we transform our old life and give our spirit a new image, we find it very hard and tiring to turn back from the darkness of earthly passions to the serene calm of the divine light.

We thus ask God to help us that a complete conversion may be brought about in us.

— Commentary on Psalm 6, 5

PRAYER. *Because of Your Name may You have mercy on me according to Your great mercy, Lord, and by no means abandon the work You have begun but complete what is imperfect in me.* *— Confessions 10, 4*

MARCH 21

Christ's Cross Abides Forever

THE saving serpent in Moses' time was fashioned from bronze as a symbol of faith in the enduring effects of the Lord's Passion. Faith in Christ's cross abides forever; it is as enduring as bronze.

Despite the constant cycle of birth and death, the cross continues to be held high above the earth for the healing of all who gaze upon it.

— Commentary on Galatians 22

PRAYER. *How great was Your love for us, kind Father! You did not spare Your only-begotten Son but surrendered Him for the sake of us sinners!* *— Confessions 10, 43*

MARCH 22

Life through Death

NLESS the Word of God had first assumed our mortal flesh He could not have died for us. Only in that way was the immortal God able to die and to give life to mortal humans.

Therefore, by this double sharing He brought about a wonderful exchange. We made death possible for Him, and He made life possible for us. — *Sermon 218C, 1*

PRAYER. *For Your law's sake I have kept faith with You, my Lord, since You have thought it worthwhile to lay down for me the law of mercy, to forgive me all my sins and to admonish me on other matters lest I offend You.*

— *Commentary on Psalm 129, 3*

MARCH 23

God Has Died for Us

O matter how great the promises the Lord has made us for the future, we must realize that the things He has already done for us are greater still.

Can anyone doubt that He will share His life with the Saints when He has already given them His death? — *Sermon 218C, 1*

PRAYER. *Lord, I have waited for You to come and deliver me from every need, for in my need You have not forsaken Your law of mercy.*

— *Commentary on Psalm 129, 3*

MARCH 24
The Glory of the Cross

ET us declare that Christ was crucified for our sake, proclaiming it with joy and pride, not with fear and shame. Paul the Apostle saw in this reason for boasting.

He could have told us many great and holy things about Christ: how as God He shared with His Father the work of creation, and how as man like us He was master of the world. But Paul would not glory in any of these wonderful things.

— *Sermon 218C, 1*

PRAYER. *Lord, in case I would falter, You gave me a remedy through Your admonishments. You established the law of forgiveness, so that as I forgive I may be forgiven.*

— *Commentary on Psalm 129, 3*

MARCH 25
Hail, Full of Grace

MARY, when Jesus was conceived in you, He found you a virgin; after being born of you He left you a virgin. He gives you fertility, but He does not violate your integrity. Whence does this happen to you? . . .

Tell me, angel Gabriel, whence this happens to Mary. The angel answers: "I stated this with my greeting, 'Hail, full of grace.'" — *Sermon 291, 6*

PRAYER. *O Mary, you were a virgin in conceiving, in bearing your child, and in dying. Pray for us to the Lord.* — *The Instruction of Beginners, 22, 40*

MARCH 26

Acknowledging Sins against Others

ALL of us have become members of Christ. How do you fail to sin against Christ when you sin against a member of Christ? Thus, if you are offering your gift at the altar and there remember that your brother or sister has anything against you, leave your gift before the altar.

God seeks you rather than your gift. Christ seeks the one whom He has redeemed by His Blood rather than what you have found in your storeroom. — *Sermon 82, 4-5*

PRAYER. *Lord, You are my refuge from the torment of the sins with which my heart besieges me. My joy is in You. Redeem me from the sorrow that my sins cause me.*

— *Commentary on Psalm 31 (1), 7*

MARCH 27

Restraining Fleshly Desires

BE sure that we will soon celebrate the passion of our crucified Lord. It is therefore in keeping with our commitment to Him that we should crucify ourselves by restraining the desires of the flesh.

Such is the cross upon which we Christians must continually hang, since our whole lives are beset by trials and temptations. — *Sermon 205, 1*

PRAYER. *Lord, You are my helper that I may dwell in Your love, my redeemer that You may deliver me from my wrongdoing.*

— *Commentary on Psalm 18 (2), 16*

MARCH 28

The Lesson of Three Crosses

STANDING in one place were three crosses. On one of them hung the thief who was
to be freed. On another hung the thief who
was to be condemned. In the middle hung
Christ Who was going to free the one and condemn the other.

What has more resemblance than these crosses? Yet what has less resemblance than the three
who hung upon them! — *Letter 93, 8*

PRAYER. *Give us, Lord, Your Christ. Let us see
Your Christ, not as His contemporaries saw Him
and crucified Him but as the angels see Him and
rejoice.* — *Commentary on Psalm 74, 11*

MARCH 29

The Nails of Christ

FLESH means the desires of our lower nature; nails signify the demands of God's
justice and holiness. With these the fear of
the Lord pierces our flesh and fastens us
to the cross as an acceptable sacrifice to Him.

In a similar passage Paul the Apostle appeals
to us by the mercy of God to offer our bodies as
a living sacrifice, holy and acceptable to God.

— *Sermon 205, 1*

PRAYER. *Do not despise me, O God my salvation, nor reject me as a mortal daring to seek
eternity. You, O God, heal the wound of my sin!*

— *Commentary on Psalm 26 (1), 9*

MARCH 30

Fraternal Correction

MY advice is that we love in every way our brothers and sisters who have committed sin. Then when it is necessary let us apply discipline. Otherwise the evil may grow by the relaxing of discipline.

If the sin is private, correct the sinner in private. If it is public, and manifest, apply the correction in public so that the sinner may be led to betterment and others may conceive a salutary fear.
— *Sermon 83, 8*

PRAYER. *Lord, let each of us, according to our conscience, either grieve in correction or rejoice in approval.* — *Commentary on Psalm 31 (2), 1*

MARCH 31

The Sacrifice of Christ

EVEN though the man Christ Jesus, in the form of God together with the Father with whom He is one God, accepts our sacrifice, nonetheless He has chosen in the form of a servant to be the sacrifice rather than to accept it.

Therefore, He is the priest Himself Who presents the offering, and He Himself is what is offered.
— *City of God, 10, 20*

PRAYER. *Lord, You gladdened my mind with spiritual joy. How glorious is Your cup, surpassing all previous delights!*
— *Commentary on Psalm 22, 5*

APRIL 1

The crucifixion Is Always Lived

THE crucifixion is something that must continue throughout our life, not for forty days only, although Moses, Elijah, and Christ fasted for forty days.

We are meant to learn from them not to cling to this present world or imitate its ways, but to nail our unregenerate selves to the cross.

— *Sermon 205, 1*

PRAYER. *Lord, we give You thanks for Your mercy. You wanted to die so that someone should rise from the dead. And someone, not anyone, but truth rose from the dead.*

— *Commentary on Psalm 147, 17*

APRIL 2

The Importance of Intention

HOW great a good was conferred on humankind by the handing over of Christ! God had in His thoughts our salvation by which we are redeemed; Judas had in his thoughts the price for which he sold the Lord.

The Son Himself had in His thoughts the price He gave for us, while Judas had in his the price he received to sell Him. The diverse intention, therefore, makes the things done diverse.

— *Sermon on 1 John 7, 8*

PRAYER. *Because of our sins we are in darkness; but You, my God, will illuminate my darkness.*

— *Commentary on Psalm 17, 29*

APRIL 3

Head and Members Pray

OD could give no greater gift to us than to make His Word, through Whom He created all things, our Head and to join us to Him as His members.

Thus, when we speak to God in prayer we do not separate the Son from Him, and when the body of the Son prays it does not separate its Head from itself. — *Commentary on Psalm 85, 1*

PRAYER. *May He perfect His gifts in us, since He did not hesitate to take our faults on Himself. And may He make us children of God, since He chose to become the child of human beings for us.* — *Sermon 184, 3*

APRIL 4

The Human Cry of Jesus

HRIST intended to teach us what we should spurn in this life and what we should hope for in the next.

Thus at the very height of His passion, when His enemies thought they had won such a mighty victory, He gave voice to our human weakness that was being crucified together with our former selves to set our sinful bodies free. And His cry was: "My God, My God, why have You forsaken Me?" — *Letter 140, 15*

PRAYER. *Let my heart praise You and my tongue say: "Lord, who is like You?" Then may You tell my soul: "I am your salvation."*

— *Confessions 9, 1*

APRIL 5

God First Loved Us

ULFILL the commandments out of love. Could anyone refuse to love our God, so abounding in mercy, so just in all His ways? Could anyone deny love to Him Who first loved us despite all our injustice and all our pride?

Could anyone refuse to love the God Who so loved us as to send His only Son not only to live among human beings but also to be put to death for their sake and at their own hands?

— *Catechetical Instructions 39*

PRAYER. *You, the Omnipotent and Good, care for each of us as if each was Your sole care, and for all as for one alone!* — *Confessions 3, 11*

APRIL 6

Without Christ We Can Do Nothing

UR Lord had the power to lay down His life and to take it up again. But we cannot choose how long we shall live, and death comes to us even against our will. Christ, by dying, has already overcome death. Our freedom from death comes only through His death.

To save us Christ had no need of us. Yet without Him we can do nothing. He gave Himself to us as the vine to the branches; apart from Him we cannot live. — *Sermons on John 84, 2*

PRAYER. *Lord, You have saved my soul from the constraint of fear, so that it may serve You in the freedom of love.* — *Commentary on Psalm 30 (1), 8*

APRIL 7

Our Human Weakness Overcome in Christ

AS evening drew near, the Lord yielded up His soul upon the cross in the certainty of receiving it back again. It was not wrested from Him against His will.

But we too were represented there. Christ had nothing to hang upon the cross except the body He had received from us. And in doing so He nailed our human weakness to the cross.

— *Commentary on Psalm 140, 5*

PRAYER. *Rise up, Lord, help us, and redeem us because of Your Name. Redeem me out of Your kindness and not for any merit of mine.*

— *Commentary on Psalm 43, 26*

APRIL 8

God Makes Me Good

BEFORE any good merits of mine, the mercy of God came to me. Even though He had found no good in me, He Himself made me good.

It is God Who justifies those who turn to Him and admonishes those who are still far away that they be converted — *Commentary on Psalm 58 (2), 2*

PRAYER. *Lord, our Mediator, God above us, human for our sake, I acknowledge Your mercy. In Your love for us You chose to be greatly troubled. Now You can much console the members of Your body who by their weakness are compelled to be troubled and to keep them from perishing in despair.* — *Sermon on John 52, 2*

APRIL 9

Made Anew

EE me in these "Confessions," that you may not praise me beyond what I am. Believe what is said of me in these, not by others but by myself. Contemplate me in these, and see what I have been, in myself and by myself.

For God has made us and not we ourselves. Indeed, we had destroyed ourselves, but He Who created us has made us anew. — *Letter 231, 6*

PRAYER. *Father, make me seek You, and save me from error. As I seek You, let nothing else come in my way in place of You.* — *Soliloquies 1, 6*

APRIL 10

Bearing One Another's Burdens

OW this is the law of Christ, that we carry one another's burdens mutually. When we love Christ, it is easy to put up with the weakness of others, even when we do not yet love them for their good qualities.

— *Eighty-three Diverse Questions 71, 7*

PRAYER. *O Lord, we are Your little flock. Keep possession of us. Spread forth Your wings and let us take shelter under them.* — *Confessions 10, 36*

APRIL 11

Bearing Our Cross

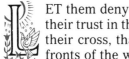 ET them deny themselves, that is, not put their trust in themselves. Let them take up their cross, that is, put up with all the affronts of the world for the love of Christ.

Persist, persevere, endure, bear up under the delay. In this way you will bear your cross.

— *Sermon 96, 9*

PRAYER. *Christ, Son of God, if You had not wished to suffer, You would not have suffered. Show us the fruit of Your passion.*

— *Commentary on Psalm 21 (2), 23*

APRIL 12

The Lesson of Nature

EALLY, is there any more marvelous sight, any occasion when human reason is nearer to some sort of converse with the nature of things, than the sowing of seeds, the planting of cuttings, the transplanting of shrubs, and the grafting of slips?

It is as though you could question the vital force in each root and bud on what it can do, and what it cannot do, and why.

— *The Literal Meaning of Genesis 8, 8*

PRAYER. *I call upon You, God, the fountain of blessings, in Whom and by Whom and through Whom all things are blessed that are blessed, in Your gracious way. Come to us.* — *Soliloquies, 1, 2*

APRIL 13

Move On

MY brothers and sisters, let us take no delights in past pleasures, and avoid being captivated by things of the present. Let us not act like a stubborn snake that stops up its ears with its tail.

Let nothing of the past prevent us from listening, and let no present things hinder us from giving thought to the future. Move on to what lies ahead. — *Commentary on Psalm 66, 10*

PRAYER. *Lord, I went astray, and then I remembered You. I heard Your voice behind me calling me to return. Now I return with excitement and desire to Your fountain.* — *Confessions 12, 10*

APRIL 14

Cross and Resurrection

JESUS' cross is an example of painful toil. His resurrection is the reward of painful toil.

In the cross He showed us how we are to bear suffering. In His resurrection He showed us what we are to hope for. — *On the Creed 3, 9*

PRAYER. *You come, O Christ, humble in appearance. You were scorned, whipped, crucified, and killed. Yet on the third day You rose again, and on the fortieth day You ascended into heaven, where You sit at the right hand of the Father and where no human being sees You.*

— *Commentary on Psalm 53, 4*

APRIL 15
Christ Died That You May Live

FOR you Christ allowed Himself to be crucified, to teach you humility. He was alive, and you were dead. He died that you might live.

God vanquished death so that death might not overcome human beings.

— Sermon on John 2, 4; 14, 13

PRAYER. Death, where is your strife? Death, where is your sting? Lord, You were struck, wounded, and cast down; but you were wounded for me, You Who made me. Death, O Death, He Who made me was wounded for me, and by His own death He conquered you. *— Sermon 128, 10*

APRIL 16
Christ's Resurrection

KNOW that our faith is strengthened by the resurrection of Christ. The passion of Christ represents the misery of our present life, while the resurrection of Christ gives us a brilliant glimpse of the happiness of the future life.

Let us apply ourselves energetically in the present life, and hope in the future. Now is the time for the painful struggle; then will come the recompense. Those who are lazy about carrying out their work will be brazenly impudent if they expect the recompense. *— Sermon 233, 1*

PRAYER. O death, when you seized my Lord, you then lost your grip on me. *— Sermon 233, 5*

APRIL 17

Be an Ant of God

MULATE the tiny ant; be an ant of God. Listen to the word of God and hide it in your heart. Collect plenty of food during the happy days of your spiritual summers.

You will then be able to endure the difficult days of temptations during the winters of your soul. — *Sermon 38, 6*

PRAYER. *Lord, You are delightful food for the pure of heart* — *Confessions 13, 21*

APRIL 18

The Kiss of Peace

IRECTLY after the Our Father, the words "Peace be with you" are said at Mass. A great sacrament lies in this kiss of peace. Let your kiss be the expression of a true love.

Do not be Judas! Judas kissed Christ with his lips, while in his heart he was already plotting against Him. — *Sermon 229, 3*

PRAYER. *Lord God, give us peace—for You have given us all things—the peace of rest, the peace of the sabbath, the sabbath that has no evening.*
— *Confessions 13, 35*

APRIL 19

Give What You Have

TO give you all the bread that you can touch and see is something that I cannot do. But this word is your portion. I give you the nourishment on which I myself subsist.

I am your fellow servant, not the father of the household. — *Sermon 339, 4*

PRAYER. *We did not exist when we were predestined, we were hostile when we were called, and we were sinners when we were justified. Then let us give thanks to God and not remain ungrateful.*
— *Sermon 158, 3*

APRIL 20

Our Brother in Heaven

WONDERFUL is the fact that, even though Christ ascended above the heavens, He remains close to those who are still living on earth. Who is this One Who is so far away and yet so near?

He is the One Who out of merciful goodness became our Brother! — *Sermon 171, 1*

PRAYER. *"That I might gaze upon the delight of the Lord": see what I love, see why I want to live in the house of the Lord all the days of my life. In it lies something wonderful to see, the delight of the Lord Himself awaiting our contemplation.*

— *Commentary on Psalm 26 (2), 8*

APRIL 21

Life—the Intermediate State

A S a torrent gathers together from the rains, and overflows, roars, runs, and by running hastens down until it finally finishes its course, so is it with our mortal life.

This human race is collected together from hidden sources and flows on, and at death travels again to hidden places. This intermediate state that is life roars and passes away.

— *Commentary on Psalm 109, 20*

PRAYER. *Behold, O Lord, we are Your little flock; we belong to You.* — *Confessions 10, 36*

APRIL 22

Inner Conflict

C ONTROLLING my will as he did, the enemy fashioned a chain out of it and bound me with it. A new will that had begun in me, to wish freely to worship You and find joy in You, O God, was not yet able to overcome that prior will, grown strong with age.

Thus did my two wills—the one old, the other new, the first carnal, the second spiritual—struggle with one another, and by their conflict they laid waste my soul. — *Confessions 8, 5*

PRAYER. *"You have proved my heart, Lord, and visited me by night": because my heart itself has been proved by the visitation of distress.*

— *Commentary on Psalm 16,3*

APRIL 23
The Choice Is God's

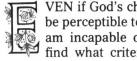EVEN if God's choice in this matter should be perceptible to some, I must admit that I am incapable of knowing. I just cannot find what criterion to apply in deciding which persons should be chosen to be saved by grace

I would instinctively choose those with better intelligence or less sins, or both; I should add, I suppose, a sound and proper education. And as soon as I decide on that, He will laugh me to scorn. — *To Simplicianus 1, 2*

PRAYER. *Lord, You value us, caring for us so much and thinking so much of us. You set us in order and know where to place us in the hierarchy of being.* — *Commentary on Psalm 143, 10*

APRIL 24
Turn Your Steps Homeward

LET us work hard every day at making progress toward God. If we are tested or tempted in our children or in our purses, let's not panic but place our hope in God. We are Christians, and our homeland is not here. Like good children, let us turn our steps homeward, that our course may be approved and guided to its conclusion. — *Sermon 16A, 13*

PRAYER. *Heal and open my eyes, Lord, that I may recognize Your will. Put to flight my foolishness that I may know You.* — *Soliloquies 1, 1*

APRIL 25

Christ's Example

 UR Lord came down from life to suffer death; the Bread came down, to hunger; the Way came down, on the way to weariness; the Font came down, to thirst.

Do you refuse to take work upon yourself? You must not seek what is for yourself; preach the truth! That is how you will come to eternity, and there find security. — *Sermon 78, 6*

PRAYER. *Lord, You strengthened me because I took refuge in You. And I took refuge because You freed me.* — *Commentary on Psalm 17, 3*

APRIL 26

We Call Upon You

INCE Christ has called, let Him be called upon. Say to Him: You have called us; we call upon You. We have understood Your vocation; hear our invocation.

Bring us to where You have promised. Perfect what You have begun. Do not abandon Your own gifts; do not abandon Your own field. Let Your plants enter Your barn!

— *Sermon on John 40, 10*

PRAYER. *"Do not abandon me, and do not despise me, God my Savior": And do not despise a mortal for daring to seek eternity. For You, O God, heal the wounds of my sin.*

— *Commentary on Psalm 26 (1), 9*

APRIL 27
Love Your Brothers and Sisters

EG God for the gift to love one another. Love all people, even your enemies, not because they are your brothers and sisters but that they may become such.

Love them in order that you may be at all times on fire with love, whether toward those who have become your brothers and sisters or toward your enemies, so that by being beloved they may become your brothers and sisters.

— *Sermon on 1 John 10, 7*

PRAYER. *To those who love You, O Lord, according to Your command, You show Yourself and You are all they seek. Thus they do not fall away from You nor back into themselves.*

— *Sermon 261, 1*

APRIL 28
Abiding in Christ

JESUS recommended to us His Body and Blood in bread and wine, elements that are reduced into one out of many constituents. What is meant by eating that food and taking that drink is this: to remain in Christ and have Him remaining in us. — *Sermon on John 26, 11*

PRAYER. *You are my strength, O Lord, so that I may stand firm in this world against all temptation. But if there are many who trouble me, You are my refuge."* — *Commentary on Psalm 70 (1), 5*

APRIL 29
Possessed by the Lord

PLEASE understand: the resurrection of the body will be an end without end. The body will die no more, will experience no more sufferings, no more hunger and thirst, and no more afflictions. Neither will it become aged or ill.

We shall be possessed by the Lord—His inheritance, and He will be ours.   *— Sermon 213, 9*

PRAYER. I have lifted up my soul to You, O Lord, as if I carried a jug to a fountain. Fill me, then, since I have lifted up my soul to You.

— Commentary on Psalm 142, 15

APRIL 30
The Beauty of Creation

YOU, Lord, created heaven and earth. They are beautiful because You are beauty. They are good because You are goodness. They exist because You are existence.

However, they are not as beautiful or as good as You, nor do they have existence as You their Creator have it. Compared with You they are neither beautiful nor good, nor do they exist.

— Confessions 11, 4

PRAYER. My God, I shall run to another to be refreshed if I have been made by another. You are all I possess, because You are my God. You are not only the giver of my inheritance, but the inheritance itself.   *— Commentary on Psalm 142, 17*

MAY 1

Forgive—Give

DO you wish to receive? Then give! Do you wish to be forgiven? Then forgive! This is just a brief summary. Hear Christ say in another place, "forgive, and you shall be forgiven."

Forgive; give. And you shall be given what you desire—eternal life. — *Sermon 64, 5*

PRAYER. *Forgive us, Lord, all these things in which we have been led astray. Help us to resist being led away.*

— *Punishment and the Forgiveness of Sins 2, 4*

MAY 2

The Following of Christ

COME, follow Me, says the Lord. Do you love? He has hastened on, He has flown on ahead. Look and see where.

O Christian, don't you know where your Lord has gone? I ask you: Don't you wish to follow Him there? Through trials, insults, the cross, and death. Why do you hesitate? Look, the way has been shown you. — *Sermon 345, 6*

PRAYER. *O Lord my God, You alone do I love. You alone do I follow. You alone do I seek. You alone am I prepared to serve, for You alone justly rule, and under Your authority I long to be.*

— *Soliloquies 1, 15*

MAY 3

How To Love God

NITE with the good—whom you will easily find if you are the same yourself—to worship and love God together without recompense. For He Himself will be all our reward, so that in the life to come we may enjoy His goodness and beauty.

However, we must love Him not as something we see with our eyes, but as we love wisdom, truth, sanctity, righteousness, charity, and the like, not as they appear in us but as they exist in the very source of incorruptible and unchangeable wisdom. — *The Instruction of Beginners 27, 55*

PRAYER. *O God, You are our only certain delight.* — *Confessions 8, 5*

MAY 4

Christian Grief for a Saintly Mother

ENTLY, I closed my mother's eyes. An immeasurable sorrow flowed up into my heart and would have overflowed in tears. But my eyes, under the mind's strong constraint, held back their flow.

As my mother breathed her last, the child Adeodatus broke out into lamentations. We checked him and brought him to silence.

— *Confessions 9, 12*

PRAYER. *Lord, I know that my mother always forgave others with all her heart. Please forgive her, too,* — *Confessions 9, 13*

70

MAY 5

Solace in God

ITTLE by little, after my mother's death, I began to recover my former feeling about Your handmaid. I remembered how loving and devout was her conversation with You and how pleasant and considerate her conversation with me, of which I was now suddenly deprived.

And I found solace in weeping in Your sight both for her and for myself. — *Confesssion 9, 12*

PRAYER. *Lord, let no one tear my mother, Monica, away from Your protection.*

— *Confessions 9, 13*

MAY 6

Prayer from the Heart

F the cry to the Lord uttered by those who pray is made with the sound of the bodily voice without the heart being turned to God, who can doubt that it is made in vain? But if it comes from the heart, even if the bodily voice is silent, it can be concealed from everyone else but not from God.

Therefore, when we pray—whether aloud as required or silently—to God, our cry must come from the heart. — *Commentary on Psalm 118 (29), 1*

PRAYER. *Lord, no heart is so closed as to shut out Your eye. Let my soul praise You that it may love You and proclaim Your mercies.*

— *Confessions 5, 1*

MAY 7
Withdrawal from God

REMEMBER this. When people choose to withdraw far from a fire, the fire continues to give warmth, but they grow cold. When people choose to withdraw far from light, the light continues to be bright in itself but they are in darkness.

This is also the case when people withdraw from God; and this is why those who praise themselves cannot praise God — *Sermon 170, 11*

PRAYER. *The human being is one of Your creatures, Lord, and its instinct is to praise You.*

— *Confessions 1, 1*

MAY 8
Spiritual Progress Draws Detractors

PEOPLE who change their way of life and begin to think about making spiritual progress also begin to suffer from the tongues of detractors.

Whoever has not yet suffered this trial has not yet made progress, and whoever is not ready to suffer it does not even endeavor to progress.

— *Commentary on Psalm 119, 3*

PRAYER. *Come to my aid, O God, the one eternal, true reality! In You there is no strife, no disorder, no change, no need, and no death; only supreme clarity, supreme permanence, supreme fullness, and supreme life.* — *Soliloquies 1, 1*

MAY 9

Love the Church—Receive the Spirit

CCORDINGLY, we too receive the Holy Spirit if we love the Church, if we are bound together by love, and if we rejoice in the Catholic name and faith.

Let us believe it, brothers and sisters: we will have the Holy Spirit in the same measure that we love the Church of Christ. Moreover, we love the Church when we stand fast in her membership and love. — *Sermon on John 32, 8*

PRAYER. *Lord, I shall hear Your voice and make haste to clasp You to myself. Do not hide Your face from me.* — *Confessions 1, 5*

MAY 10

Possessing the Scriptures

HEN you understand anything in the Scriptures, it is love that is manifesting itself to you; when you fail to understand, it is love that is hiding itself from you.

Those, therefore, who possess charity possess both what is manifest in the divine words and what is hidden in them. — *Sermon 350, 2*

PRAYER. *Lord, increase my faith, hope, and love! How wonderful and unmatched is Your goodness!* — *Soliloquies 1, 1*

MAY 11

Love Your Neighbor—Receive the Spirit

OW do we come to know that we have received the Holy Spirit? We must question our own heart. If we love our neighbor, the Spirit of God dwells in us.

We must put ourselves to the test before God by seeing if there is in us love for peace and unity and love for the Church spread throughout the world. — *Sermon on 1 John 6, 10*

PRAYER. *O Lord my God, let my soul praise You that it may love You. And let it recount to You Your mercies that it may praise You for them all.*
— *Confessions 5, 11*

MAY 12

A Foretaste of Heavenly Beauty

NVISION the extraordinary brilliance and effects of the light in sun and moon and stars, in the dark shades of a glade, in the colors and scents of flowers. Then there is the grandeur of the spectacle of the sea as it slips on and off its many colors like robes.

All these are mere consolations for us, not the rewards of the blessed. What can such rewards be like, then, if such things here are so many, so great, and of such quality? — *City of God 22, 24*

PRAYER. *Look at the heavens and the earth: in their steady change and alteration they proclaim that they were made, and their very existence is itself the voice with which they speak. It was You, O Lord, Who created them.*
— *Confessions 9,4*

MAY 13

The Way of Charity

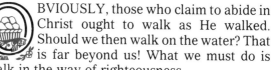 BVIOUSLY, those who claim to abide in Christ ought to walk as He walked. Should we then walk on the water? That is far beyond us! What we must do is walk in the way of righteousness.

In what way? I have already mentioned it. He was fixed upon the cross, and yet He was walking in this very way—the way of charity: "Father, forgive them; they do not know what they are doing." If, therefore, you have learned to pray for your enemy, you are walking in the way of the Lord. — *Sermon on 1 John 1, 9*

PRAYER. *Lord, show me the road I must travel that I may see You.* — *Soliloquies 1, 1*

MAY 14

Sign of Love

 NOW that those who have love are born of God; those who do not have it are not born of God. This is the distinctive sign par excellence.

No matter what else you might have, if you lack this, it profits you nothing. And no matter what else you lack, if you have this you have fulfilled the law. — *Sermon on 1 John 5, 7*

PRAYER. *O God, be my inheritance, for I love You totally. With all my heart, with all my mind, I love You.* — *Sermon 334, 3*

MAY 15

Studying the Scriptures with Humility

Y ambition as a youth was to apply to the study of the Holy Scriptures all the refinement of dialectics. I did so, but without the humility of the true searcher. I was supposed to knock at the door so that it would open for me. Instead I was pushing it closed, trying to understand in pride what is only learned in humility.

However, the all-merciful Lord lifted me up and kept me safe. — *Sermon 51, 6*

PRAYER. *O God my Father, I am seeking You, not making statements about You. Help me and guide me.* — *Confessions 9, 17*

MAY 16

Recognize Christ

HRIST is at once above and below: above in Himself, below in His people. Fear Christ above, and recognize Him below.

Here He is poor, with and in the poor; there He is rich, with and in God. Have Christ above bestowing His bounty; recognize Him here in His need. — *Sermon 123, 44*

PRAYER. *Let me know You, my Father, let me know You as I too am known. Enter my soul, You Who are its strength, and make it what You want.* — *Confessions 10, 1*

MAY 17
Never Tire of Trying

B E assured that you can never be perfect in this world unless you realize that it is impossible for you to be perfect here. Therefore, your aim in life should be as follows.

Always try your best in doing what you have to do, so that you may reach perfection. Never get tired of trying, because there is always room for improvement. — *Commentary on Psalm 33, 14*

PRAYER. *How do I seek You, O Lord? For when I seek You, it is happiness I seek. Let me seek You that my soul may live; as my body lives by my soul, so my soul lives by You.*

— *Confessions 10, 20*

MAY 18
Value of Augustine's "Confessions"

T HE thirteen books of my "Confessions" are intended to praise the just and good God in all my evil as well as good ways and to stir up toward Him the mind and feelings of human beings. As far as I am concerned, they had this effect on me when I wrote them, and they still do so when I read them.

What others think is their own business. I know that many of the brothers and sisters have enjoyed them, and still do so. — *Revisions 2, 32*

PRAYER. *Lord, I give You an account of so many things to excite my own love and that of my readers for You, that we all may say: "The Lord is great and exceedingly to be praised."*

— *Confessions 11, 1*

MAY 19

Thanks Be to You

HOW magnificent are Your works; in wisdom You have made them all. Thanks be to You! But You have made us over all of them. Thanks be to You!

When we despised You, we were not despised: in case we should have forgotten Your Divinity and should lose You, *You* even took upon Yourself our humanity. Thanks be to You! When and where can there not be thanks? — *Sermon 16A, 6*

PRAYER. Lord, Your best servants are those who wish to shape their life on Your answers rather than shape Your answers on their wishes.

— *Confessions 10, 26*

MAY 20

Christ Has Put an End to Fear

DID not Peter deny Christ out of fear of being put to death? By His resurrection Christ took away that fear of death. And because He had taken away fear of death, He asked, as was proper, if Peter loved Him.

Fear had denied Christ three times. Three times love confessed Him. A threefold negation, the desertion or truth; a threefold confession, the witness of love. — *Sermon 147, 3*

PRAYER. I call upon You, my God, my Mercy, my Creator. I had forgotten You, but You held me ever in Your sight. — *Confessions 13, 1*

MAY 21

The Right Hand of the Father

JESUS ascended into heaven. And where is He now? He sits at the right hand of the Father. Do you know what "the right hand" means?'

"The right hand of God" means eternal happiness. It means inestimable, inexpressible, incomprehensible beatitude.

— *Sermon 213, 4*

PRAYER. *Let Your right hand save me, O Lord, let it save me, so that I may stand on Your right hand. I ask not health of body but that having finished the present life I may be found on Your right hand among the sheep.*

— *Commentary on Psalm 59, 7*

MAY 22

Christ Is Our Way

LISTEN to Christ: Do you wish to walk? I am the Way. Do you wish not to be deceived? I am the Truth. Do you wish not to die? I am the Life.

There is no place for you to go except to Me. There is no manner of going except through Me.

— *Sermon on John 22, 8*

PRAYER. *Lord, let me walk along the path of sublimity with the feet of humility.*

— *Holy Virginity, 52, 53*

MAY 23

The Path of Christ

UNDOUBTEDLY, the path of Christ seems hard, but it is the safe way. Another path may hold out pleasures, but it is also teeming with robbers.

— *Commentary on Psalm 36 (2), 16*

PRAYER. *Be my helper, and do not abandon me. See, I am on Your path. I have asked for only one thing from You: to live in Your house all the days of my life, to gaze upon Your delight, and to be protected in Your temple. One thing I have asked for, but to attain it I am on Your path.*

— *Commentary on Psalm 26 (2), 17*

MAY 24

Love, and Do What You Will

ONCE and for all, a short rule is laid down for you: Love, and do what you will. If you keep silence, do it out of love. If you cry out, do it out of love. If you refrain from punishing, do it out of love

Let the root of love be within. From such a root nothing but good can come.

— *Sermon on 1 John 7, 8*

PRAYER. *I love You alone, Lord. I seek You alone. I yearn to be possessed by You alone.*

— *Soliloquies 1, 1*

MAY 25
Seek What Is Better

SEEK what is better than you are so that you can be made better by it. If you desire gold, you may or may not obtain it. But you can always possess God whenever you wish.

Desire God so that you may have Him, and then finally you will be really happy. This alone will make you truly happy. Love this, possess this; you can have this when you wish and without cost. — *Commentary on Psalm 32, 16*

PRAYER. My faith, O Lord, which You gave me through the humanity of Your Son, calls upon You. — *Confessions 1, 1*

MAY 26
Spiritual Power of the Sacrament

PROUD ministers are reckoned with the devil. But the gift of Christ, which is pure and flows through them, is not thereby contaminated.

For the spiritual power of the Sacrament is just like light. It is pure and is received by those who are to be enlightened. Nor does it become less pure even though it passes through unclean ministers. — *Sermon on John 5, 5*

PRAYER. Let them listen to You, O kind Jesus, and come to You. Let them learn from You to be meek and humble, since they need Your mercy and Your truth to live for You and not for themselves. — *Holy Virginity, 36, 36*

MAY 27
The Holy Spirit Animates Us

WHAT the soul is to the human body the Holy Spirit is to the Body of Christ, the Church. The Holy Spirit is active in the whole Church in the same way that the soul animates all the members of the human body. — *Sermon 267, 4*

PRAYER. *Let me know You, O You Who know me. Let me know You just as I am known to You. Virtue of my soul, come into it and make it over for Your own use, that You may possess it without spot or wrinkle. This is my hope.*

— *Confessions 10, 1*

MAY 28
Gossipers Stir Up Disharmony

GOSSIPERS are described in a certain passage of the Scriptures this way: "The heart of the fool is as the wheel of the cart." It carries hay, and creeks, and keeps on creaking without end. Thus there are many brothers and sisters who do not dwell together except physically.

What type of people do dwell together? People about whom it can be said: "They have one mind and one heart in the service of God."

— *Commentary on Psalm 132, 8*

PRAYER. *Remember me, O Lord, not according to Your wrath, which I have deserved, but according to Your mercy. This befits You, O Lord, not owing to my merit but to Your kindness.*

— *Commentary on Psalm 24, 7*

MAY 29
Spiritual Growth through Temptations

EARTHLY life is a pilgrimage, and as such it is full of temptations. But our spiritual growth is worked out in temptation.

By experiencing temptations, we know ourselves. By fighting them, we have the chance to become winners. By overcoming them, we are crowned victors — *Commentary on Psalm 80, 3*

PRAYER. Lord, You are our Physician, healing the ills of all. You reduce the swelling of pride, renew wasted life, and excise what is superfluous. You preserve what is necessary, restore what has been lost, and cure what has been corrupted. — *Christian Combat, 11, 12*

MAY 30
In Heaven But Still on Earth

OUR Head about to ascend to heaven commended to us His members on earth. To Saul the persecutor He said from on high: "Saul, Saul, why do you persecute Me?"

That is, I have ascended to heaven, but I still remain on earth; here I sit at the right hand of the Father, but there I still hunger, thirst and am a stranger. — *Sermon on 1 John 10, 9*

PRAYER. Lord, You perfected my love, that I might surmount the troublesome entanglements of this world. Direct my desire toward the heavenly home so that I may be enriched with every good thing. — *Commentary on Psalm 17, 34*

MAY 31
Eat Life—Drink Life

NLESS you eat My Flesh and drink My Blood, you shall not have life in you," says the Lord. Eat life—drink life. You will then have life, and life is complete.

Then the Body and Blood of Christ will be life for each person, under this condition: what is eaten visibly in the Sacrament be spiritually eaten and spiritually drunk in truth itself.

— *Sermon 131, 1*

PRAYER. *Give Yourself to me, O my God, for I love You. And if that is not enough, let me love You more ardently.* — *Confessions 13, 8*

JUNE 1
Head in Heaven, Body on Earth

ASCENDING into heaven on the fortieth day, our Lord Jesus Christ commended to us His Body where it would continue to lie, because He saw that many would honor Him for His ascent into heaven.

He saw that their honoring Him is useless if they trample upon His members who are here on earth. And lest anyone should err in this regard, He told us that His members would be here.

— *Sermon on 1 John 10, 9*

PRAYER. *Be a protecting God for me. I will not be saved unless it is in You. Unless you were my rest, my sickness would not be healed. Lift me up from the ground. Let me lie on You so that I may arise in a fortified place.*

— *Commentary on Psalm 70 (1), 5*

JUNE 2

Christians in Name Only

ANY call themselves Christian, but that they certainly are not! They are not what their title signifies—not in their life, not in their morals, not in their faith, not in their hope, and not in their charity.
— *Sermon on 1 John 4, 4*

PRAYER. *Lord, my God, I am helpless and poor, but You are generous to all who call upon You, and You take complete care of us. Guard my lips, both those of my body and those of my mind, from any rashness and from any lie.*

— *Confessions 11, 2*

JUNE 3

God, Creator of Rich and Poor

OD made both the rich and the poor. So the rich and the poor are born alike. You meet one another as you walk on the way together. Do not oppress or defraud anyone.

One may be needy and another may have plenty. But the Lord is the maker of them both. Through the person who has, He helps the one who needs; and through the person who does not have, He tests the one who has.   — *Sermon 35, 7*

PRAYER. *Lord, You are the light of my heart and the bread in the mouth of my soul! You are the virtue dwelling in my mind and the hiding place of my thoughts!*   — *Confessions 1, 13*

JUNE 4
Pride Can Destroy

PARADOXICALLY, it is good, in a way, for those who observe continence and are proud of it to fall, so that they may be humbled in that very thing on which they pride themselves. What benefit is continence for us if pride holds sway over our lives?

A humble married woman is to be preferred to a proud virgin. — *Sermon 354, 9*

PRAYER. *Lord, my God, how great You are, and You make Your home in the humble of heart! It is You Who lift up the downtrodden, and You are their grandeur.* — *Confessions 11, 31*

JUNE 5
The Gift of Celibacy

THOSE to whom the gift of celibacy is not given either are unwilling or do not fulfill their will, whereas those to whom it is given order their will in such a way as to accomplish what they wish.

In order, therefore, that this message, which is not received by all persons, may yet be received by some, God's grace and their free will combine in securing to them the gift.

— *Grace and Free Will, 1, 4*

PRAYER. *Lord, You truly gave me free will, but without You my effort is worthless. You give help since You are the One Who created, and You do not abandon Your creation.*

— *Commentary on Psalm 26 (2), 17*

JUNE 6
Gift for the Clergy

REALIZE, my brothers and sisters, that if you wish to give anything to the clerics, you are not to do so in such a way as to add fire to their vices, acting against me.

Offer whatever you wish to the community as a whole; offer of your own goodwill. What is in the common store will be distributed to each according to need.
— *Sermon 356, 13*

PRAYER. *You, Who always are, both before we were and before the world existed, have become for us a refuge in which we have turned to You.*
— *Commentary on Psalm 89, 3*

JUNE 7
The Catholic Church

WE are the holy Church. But I do not say "we" as though to indicate only we who are here, you who have just been listening to me. I mean all of us who are here and by the grace of God faithful Christians in this church, that is, in this city; all those in this region, in this province, across the sea, all those in the whole world.

Such is the Catholic Church, our true mother, the true spouse of so great a husband.

— *Sermon 213, 7*

PRAYER. *O Body of Christ, holy Church, let all your bones say, "Lord, who is there like You?"*
— *Commentary on Psalm 34, 14*

JUNE 8

The Spirit Gives Life

YOU have received the law, and you wished to keep it but were unable to do so. You have fallen through pride, and you realized your weakness. Run to the Physician and wash your face.

Long for Christ, confess Christ, and believe in Christ. The Spirit will be added to the letter, and you will be saved. If you take away the Spirit the letter kills, and then what hope will remain? But the Spirit gives life. — *Sermon 136, 5*

PRAYER. *O Truth, light of my life, let me not be my own life for I lived badly on my own power and was deadly to myself. In You, however, I live again.* — *Confessions 12, 10*

JUNE 9

The Spirit of Love

EXCELLENT guest that He is, the Spirit finds you empty and fills you; He finds you hungry and thirsty and satisfies you abundantly.

God the Holy Spirit, Who comes from God, when He enters into people, draws them to the love of God and neighbor. Indeed, He is love itself. — *Sermon 225, 4*

PRAYER. *Cling to the Lord with love, that your life may grow in the last days. Hold fast as well to the faithful, great, certain, and everlasting promises of God, and to the unshakable and ineffable gift of His forbearance.* — *Letter 248, 1*

JUNE 10
Receive What You Are

NOW when you receive communion, you receive the mystery of your own communion in love. Being many, you are one body. Many grapes hang on the vine, but the juice of grapes is mingled into oneness.

Therefore, be what you see, and receive what you are.
— *Sermon 272*

PRAYER. *O Sacrament of love, sign of our unity and bond of our fraternity, all who long for life have here its very source! Let them come here and believe; unite with You and live.*

— *Sermons on John 26, 13*

JUNE 11
Sing and March

COME, my brothers and sisters, let us sing. Not for our delights, as we rest, but to cheer us in our labor. As pilgrims on the way, sing in hope, but keep on marching.

Are we making progress in good works, in true faith, in right living? We are in the right way. So don't rest for the sake of singing, but sing and march in the hope of eternal rest. — *Sermon 256, 3*

PRAYER. *As long as we are here, let us ask God not to deprive us of our prayer and His mercy, so that we may pray with perseverance and He may have mercy with perseverance.*

— *Commentary on Psalm 65, 24*

JUNE 12

The Call of Augustine to Ministry

I, WHOM you see, with God's grace, as your bishop—I came as a young man to this city. I did what I could to seek salvation in a humble position rather than be in danger in high office. But a slave may not contradict his Lord.

I came to this city to see a friend. I felt secure, for the place already had a bishop. I was seized. I was made a priest, and from there I became your bishop. — *Sermon 355,2*

PRAYER. *Heal and open my eyes that I may recognize Your will. Put to flight my foolishness that I may know You.* — *Soliloquies 1, 1*

JUNE 13

The Church Cries Out for Help

SCATTERED about the entire earth, your mother the Church is tormented by the assaults of error. She is also afflicted by the laziness and indifference of so many of the children she carries around in her bosom as well as by the sight of so many of her members growing cold, while she becomes less able to help her little ones.

Who then will give her the necessary help she cries for if not other children and other members to whose number you belong? — *Letter 243, 8*

PRAYER. *O Lord my God, pay heed to my prayer. Look with mercy on my desire, which is not concerned with myself alone but with my neighbor's good as well.* — *Confessions 11, 2*

JUNE 14
The Spirit Within

BROTHERS and sisters, we are part of one Body, and we have one Head, in heaven. Our two physical eyes do not see one another, but they know each other in virtue of the love that knits them together. Together they meet in and are directed to one object. Their aim is one; their places are diverse.

If then all who with you love God have one aim with you, it is of no significance that in the Body you are separated in place. You have the eyesight of your heart fixed alike on the light of truth.
— Sermon on 1 John 6, 10

PRAYER. *I ask You, my God, to reveal me to myself.*
— Confessions 10, 1

JUNE 15

The Body of Christ

YOUR Lord is seated at the Father's right hand in heaven. How then is the bread His Body? And the chalice, or rather its content, how is it His Blood?
These elements are called Sacraments, because in them one thing is perceived by the senses and another thing by the mind. What is seen has a bodily appearance; what the mind perceives produces spiritual fruit. You hear the words "The Body of Christ," and you answer "Amen."
— Sermon 272

PRAYER. *O food and bread of angels, the angels take their fill of You. They are satisfied by You but never tire of You.*
— Sermon 196, 13

JUNE 16
Awake Christ Sleeping in You

FACE the world as you face a tumultuous and tempestuous sea. Sail across this world in the boat of your interior peacefulness, without losing sight of the harbor.

When the strong winds of its desires try to take hold of you, call for help and awake Christ sleeping in the cabin of your heart. — *Sermon 76, 9*

PRAYER. *I desire You, O justice and innocence, beautiful and comely with luminous clarity and unquenchable satisfaction. With you there is profound rest and untroubled life. All who enter into You enter into joy.* — *Confessions 2, 10*

JUNE 17
The Sea-Walker

LOOK at the acrobat. There you have a person who at great pains has learned to walk on a tightrope and by being suspended keeps you in suspense. But now turn your gaze toward Him Who does far more spectacular things. Did He learn to walk on a tightrope? No! He walked on the sea!

Forget your theater, then, for a moment and fix your gaze on Him Who is our "Rock." No tightrope-walker is He, but a sea-walker.

— *Commentary on Psalm 55, 4*

PRAYER. *Alas for me, O Lord, how high You are in the heights, and how deep in the depths! Nowhere do You withdraw, yet we scarcely return to You!* — *Confessions 8, 3*

JUNE 18

Not on Your Own

HERE are some people who consider themselves able to refine themselves on their own, in order to contemplate and remain in God.

Accordingly, they look down upon the mass of Christians who live on faith alone as not being yet able to do as they do.　— *The Trinity 4. 15*

PRAYER.　*Give me strength to seek You, Lord, for You have already enabled me to find You and have given me hope of finding You ever more fully.*　— *The Trinity 15, 51*

JUNE 19

Truth through Signs

RESENTATION of truth through signs has great power to feed and fan that ardent love by which, as under some law of gravitation, we flicker upward, or inward, to our place of rest.

The emotions are less easily set alight while the soul is wholly absorbed in material things. But when it is brought to material signs of spiritual realities, and moves from them to the things they represent, it gathers strength just by this very act of passing from the one to the other.

— *Letter 55, 11*

PRAYER.　*Lord, my knowledge and my ignorance lie before You. Where You have opened to me, let me enter. Where You have closed to me, open when I knock.*　— *The Trinity 15, 51*

JUNE 20
Everything Becomes Light with Love

EVEN those fasts and night watches that seem burdensome and are taken on so as not to disturb one's health are turned into spiritual pleasure—provided they are accepted with prayer, psalmody, and reading and meditation on the law of God.

The labor of those who love is in no way burdensome; in fact, it even gives pleasure. What matters is what is loved. When we do what we love, either we do not notice the work or the work itself is loved. — *Holy Widowhood, 21, 26*

PRAYER. *Lord, all that I am I am with Your mercy.* — *Sermon 16A, 6*

JUNE 21
Question Your Heart

MY brothers and sisters, question your heart, and if you cannot find love of neighbor there set your mind at ease. Such love cannot exist without the Spirit of God.

Paul the Apostle bears witness to this: "The love of God has been poured out in our hearts through the Holy Spirit Who has been given to us." — *Sermon on 1 John 6, 10*

PRAYER. *Lord, whatever You give me is too little for me. Be Yourself my inheritance! I love You without reserve: with all my heart, soul, and mind. Of what value is anything You give me that is not Yourself!* — *Sermons 334, 3*

JUNE 22
The Upright of Heart

D O you know who the upright of heart are? They are those who wish what God wishes. Therefore, do not try to twist God's will to your own but correct your will to that of God.

The will of God is a rule of conduct. By it you have the means of being converted and of correcting your evil ways.

— *Commentary on Psalm 93, 18*

PRAYER. Put to flight my foolishness, Lord, that I may know You. Show me the road I must travel that I may see You. Thus aided, I hope I shall do all You have commanded me. — *Soliloquies 1, 1*

JUNE 23
The Eucharist Forgives Sins

A CCORDINGLY, eat the bread of heaven in a spiritual way. Come to it freed from sin. Even though your sins occur daily, at least see to it that they be not mortal. Moreover, before you approach the altar note well what you say: "Forgive us our trespasses as we forgive those who trespass against us." If you forgive others, God will forgive you.

— *Sermon on John 26, 11*

PRAYER. Forgive us, Lord, all these things in which we have been led astray. Help us to resist being led away.

— *Punishment and the Forgiveness of Sins 2, 4*

JUNE 24

Humility of John the Baptist

JOHN the Baptist was regarded by some people as the Messiah but he told them: "I am not the one whom you think." He refused to accept the error of someone in order to derive glory from it.

John admitted what he was, declared what he was not, and humbled himself. He clearly recognized where his salvation came from, for he understood that he was the lamp, and he feared being extinguished by pride. — *Sermon 293, 4*

PRAYER. *Thanks and praise to You, my God, Who sound in my ears and Who illuminate my heart. Keep me away from every temptation.*

— Confessions 10, 31

JUNE 25

God the Father and Our Mother the Church

UNFLAGGINGLY, let us love the Lord our God and let us love His Church. Let us love Him as the Lord and the Church as His handmaid.

No one can offend the one and still be pleasing to the other. What does it avail you if you do not directly offend the Father but do offend the mother? — *Commentary on Psalm 88, 14*

PRAYER. *Let my mouth speak the praise of the Lord by Whom all things were made and Who was made amidst all things. He is the witness of the Father and the creator of the mother.*

— Sermon 188, 3

JUNE 26
Live from God for God

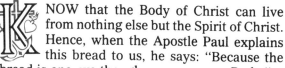

NOW that the Body of Christ can live from nothing else but the Spirit of Christ. Hence, when the Apostle Paul explains this bread to us, he says: "Because the bread is one, we though many are one Body."

O Sacrament of love! Sign of our unity! Bond of our fraternity! All who long for life have here its very source. Let them come here and believe, unite with You and live. Let them cling to the Body and live for God. — *Sermon on John 26, 11*

PRAYER. *Thanks be to Him Who is desired before He is seen, whose presence is felt and Who is hoped for in the future.* — *Sermon 24, 1*

JUNE 27
Come and Be Filled

ET us come to this Supper and be filled to satiety. And who have come to this Supper except the beggars, the sick, the lame, and the blind?

Let the beggars come, for He invites us Who became poor for our sakes. Let the sick come, for it is not the healthy who need a physician but the sick. Let the blind come and say to Him: "Give light to my eyes lest I sleep in death."

— *Sermon 112, 18*

PRAYER. *O God, come to me in Your kindness. For You are the good and the beautiful, in Whom, by Whom, and through Whom all things are good and beautiful.* — *Soliloquies 1,1*

JUNE 28

Prayer to Christ within Us

REMEMBER, there is One Who listens to you, so do not hesitate to pray to Him. But He abides within you. You need only purify the inmost recesses of your heart.

He is the Lord our God, the Word of God, the Word made human, Son of the Father, Son of God and Son of Man. — *Sermon on John 10, 1*

PRAYER. *O Word before all time, by Whom time was made, born in time although You are eternal life, You call us who are bound by time and make us eternal.* — *Commentary on Psalm 101 (2), 10*

JUNE 29

Peter, Figure of the Church

NOW if the line of bishops who succeed one another is to be considered, with how much certainty and with real advantage do we begin with Saint Peter?

He was the figure of the whole Church, and our Lord said to him: "Upon this rock I will build My Church, and the gates of hell shall not prevail against it." Thus, the certain hope of the faithful, which rests not on human beings but on God, will never be destroyed. — *Letter 53, 2-3*

PRAYER. *Lord, teach me what I should teach, teach me what I should hold fast.* — *Letter 166, 10*

JUNE 30

Act in the Proper Way

IF they are children of God, let them understand that they are moved by God so that they may do what is to be done. And when they have done it, let them give thanks to Him by Whom they do it.

Hence, when they act in the proper way, that is, with love and the delight of justice, they should rejoice that they have received the sweetness the Lord has given them. When they do not act in the proper way, let them pray that they may receive what they do not yet have.

— *Correction and Grace 4*

PRAYER. *Perfect me, O Lord.* — *Confessions 11, 2*

JULY 1

One Teacher: Christ

AVOID being called "Teacher." Only One is your teacher, the Messiah. Let Him therefore speak to you interiorly, in that place where no one can enter into your heart.

On second thought, let there not be no one in your heart—let Christ be there. Let His unction spread in your heart, lest it be a heart thirsting in the wilderness and having no fountains to be quenched. — *Sermon on 1 John 3, 13*

PRAYER. *You have accompanied me on my path, O Truth, teaching me what to avoid and what to desire.* — *Confessions 10, 40*

99

JULY 2

Love the Whole Christ

EXTEND your love over the whole earth if you desire to love Christ, for Christ's members are all over the earth. If you love but a part, you are divided. If you are divided, you are not in the Body. If you are not in the Body, you are not under the Head.

What good is it for you to believe and blaspheme Him in the Body! — *Sermon on 1 John 10, 7*

PRAYER. *Behold, O Lord, we are Your little flock. We belong to You.* — *Confessions 10, 36*

JULY 3

Who Are the Proud?

WHO are the proud? Those who do not perform penance and confess their sins in order to be healed through humility. Who are the proud? Those who attribute to themselves the few good qualities they seem to possess and endeavor to diminish the mercy of God.

Who are the proud? Those who, while attributing to God the good they accomplish, insult others for not performing such works and raise themselves above them.

— *Commentary on Psalm 93, 15*

PRAYER. *This is my glory, Lord my God, that I might proclaim to You forever that there is nothing from myself for me. All good things come from You, for You are God, all things in all.*

— *Commentary on Psalm 29, 13*

JULY 4
Let Our Lives Be Good

BAD times! Troublesome times! This is what people are saying. Let our lives be good and the times will be good. For we make our own times. Such as we are, such are the times.

What can we do? Maybe we cannot convert masses of people to a good life. But let the few who do hear live well. Let the few who live well endure the many who live badly. — *Sermon 30, 8*

PRAYER. *O Truth, light of my heart, let not my shadows speak to me. Let me not be my own life, for I lived badly on my own power and was deadly to myself. In You, however, I live again. It is You Who speak and converse with me.*

— *Confessions 12, 10*

JULY 5
Think Lowly

DO you wish to be great? Then begin from what is slightest. Do you plan to construct a high and mighty building? Then think first about the foundation of humility.

When people plan to erect a lofty and large building, they make the foundations all the deeper. But those who lay the foundation are forced to descend into the depths. — *Sermon 69, 2*

PRAYER. *Lord, my God, how great You are, and yet You make Your home in the humble of heart! It is You Who lift up the downtrodden, and You Who are their grandeur.* — *Confessions 11, 31*

JULY 6

The Love of God and the Church

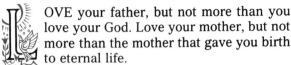

LOVE your father, but not more than you love your God. Love your mother, but not more than the mother that gave you birth to eternal life.

Furthermore, from this same love of your parents see how much you ought to love God and the Church. For if so much love is owed to those who begot you to a life that must end with your death, how much more grateful love is owed to those who begot you for an eternal destiny!

— Sermon 344, 2

PRAYER. *Cling to the Lord with love, that your life may grow in the last days. Hold fast as well to the faithful, great, certain, and everlasting promises of God and to the unshakable and ineffable gift of His forbearance.* *— Letter 248, 1*

JULY 7

Lord, Save Me

GREAT virtue is needed to struggle with happiness. We must learn to tread upon the world and remember to trust Christ. And if you begin to sin, say: "Lord, I am perishing; save me," so that you may not perish. For only He can deliver you from the death of the body, He Who died in the body for you. *— Sermon 26, 9*

PRAYER. *Lord our God, make us blessed by You, because we shall not lose You. When we remain true to You, we shall neither lose You nor be lost ourselves.* *— Sermon 113, 6*

JULY 8

The Power of Words

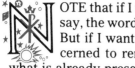 OTE that if I think of what I am going to say, the word already exists in my heart. But if I want to speak to you, I am concerned to render present to your heart what is already present in mine.

Then, seeking a way to let the word that exists in me reach you and dwell with you, I have recourse to my voice. Its sound communicates my word and its meaning to you. When it is finished it vanishes. But my word, is now in you, without ever having left me. — *Sermon 293, 3*

PRAYER. *I ask You, my God, to reveal me to myself.* — *Confessions 10, 1*

JULY 9

The Prayers of the Martyrs

T this table we do not commemorate the martyrs in the same way as we commemorate others who now rest in peace, so as to include them in our prayers. Rather, we commemorate them in order that they may pray for us and help us to follow in their steps.

The martyrs practiced that perfect love which Christ said could not be surpassed. They offered their brothers and sisters the same kind of meal as they themselves had received from the table of the Lord. — *Sermon on John 84, 2*

PRAYER. *O Body of Christ, holy Church, let all your bones say, "Lord, who is there like You?"*

— *Commentary on Psalm 34, 14*

JULY 10

See God in Your Neighbor

YOU who do not yet see God will, by loving your neighbor, make yourself worthy of seeing Him. By loving your neighbor, you cleanse your eyes so you can see God.

Love your neighbor, then, and see within yourself the source of this love of neighbor. There you will see God insofar as you are able.

— *Sermon on John 17, 8*

PRAYER. *O Lord, my God, pay heed to my prayer. Look with mercy on my desire, which is not concerned with myself alone but with my neighbor's good as well.* — *Confessions 11, 2*

JULY 11

The Toil of Righteousness

MOST people would desire—if it were possible—to obtain at once the joys of lovely and perfect wisdom, without the endurance of toil in action and suffering. However, that is impossible in this mortal life.

In the discipline of the human, the toil of doing the work precedes the delight of understanding the truth. — *Against Faustus 22, 52*

PRAYER. *Lord, You truly gave me free will, but without You my effort is worthless. You give help since You are the One Who created, and You do not abandon Your creation.*

— *Commentary on Psalm 26 (2), 17*

JULY 12
A Gradual Knowledge

SINCE the flame that was to burn us up entirely had not yet flared up, my friends and I thought that the glow emanating from Philosophy and our way of life that warmed us slowly was the greatest there could be. Suddenly some substantial books appeared and started up an incredible blaze in me. It was more powerful than I can bring myself to believe.

After this, how could honor, human pomp, desire for empty fame, or the consolations of this dying life move me! Swiftly, I turned completely in upon myself. — *Against the Academics 2, 2*

PRAYER. *You, Who always are, both before we were and before the world existed, have become for us a refuge in which we have turned to You.*

— *Commentary on Psalm 89, 3*

JULY 13
Leaders Are Servants

THE first thing good superiors must realize is that they are servants. They should not consider it beneath their dignity to be servants to many.

Indeed, the Lord of lords did not consider it beneath His dignity to be a servant to us.

— *Sermon 340A, 1*

PRAYER. *Put to flight my foolishness, Lord, that I may know You. Show me the road I must travel that I may see You. Thus aided, I hope I shall do all You have commanded me.* — *Soliloquies 1, 1*

JULY 14

Admitting One's Weakness

REMEMBER, you will be faulted not because you are ignorant against your will but because you neglect to seek out what it is that makes you ignorant.

No one has ever been deprived of the ability to know the importance of finding out what it is damaging to be ignorant of. Neither have any been deprived of the ability to know that they should confess their weakness. —*Free Will 3, 19*

PRAYER. *I have gone astray, and I have remembered You. I heard Your voice behind me calling me to return. And now I return with excitement and desire to Your fountain.* —*Confessions 12, 10*

JULY 15

Pray without Much Speaking

UNQUESTIONABLY, it is not reprehensible or useless to pray at length when one is free. This means when the obligations of other good and necessary works do not prevent us—although even then we must always pray by the aspirations of the heart.

But to pray at length does not mean, as some think, to pray with much speaking. Continual longing is not the same as much speaking.

—*Letter 130, 19*

PRAYER. *O Lord, my God, let my soul praise You that it may love You, and let it recount to You Your mercies that it may praise You for them all.*

—*Confessions 5, 1*

JULY 16

Your Good Name

ONSCIENCE and good name are but two different aspects of truthfulness. Conscience is for your own sake; good name for the sake of your neighbors.

All who are solidly established in their own conscience but do not care about their good name become callous, particularly if they are in a position of leadership. — *Sermon 355, 1*

PRAYER. *I thank You, O Lord, my joy and my glory, my hope and my God. I thank You for Your gifts to me. Keep them unharmed for me: they will be the making of me, and I shall be with You for my being is Your gift.* — *Confessions 1, 20*

JULY 17

Even in Waging War Be a Peacemaker

EACE should be the object of our desire and war looked upon as a necessity to the end that God may deliver us from the need for war and preserve us in peace. Peace is not sought in order to rouse people to war, but war is waged that peace may be obtained.

Therefore, even in waging war be a peacemaker. In this way, by conquering those whom you combat you may lead them back to the blessings of peace. — *Letter 189, 6*

PRAYER. *Lord God, give us peace—for you have given us all things—the peace of rest, the peace of the sabbath, the sabbath that has no evening.*

— *Confessions 13, 35*

JULY 18
Not by Walking But by Loving

WE approach God not by walking but by loving. The purer our love for Him toward Whom we are striving, the more present to us will He be.

To Him, therefore, Who is everywhere present and everywhere whole, we must proceed not by our feet but by our moral virtues—judged not by the object of our knowledge but by the object of our love.
— *Letter 155, 13*

PRAYER. *Let my soul rouse itself, Lord, from weariness, lean on Your creation, and hobble toward You Who made it all. For in You we are remade and find true strength.* — *Confessions 5, 1*

JULY 19
Special Times for Prayer

LET us desire continually, and thus let us pray continually. But at certain hours we ought to recall our minds from other cares and business, in which desire itself is almost somehow cooled down, to the very business of prayer.

We must admonish ourselves by the words of our prayer to fix attention upon that which we desire.
— *Letter 130, 10*

PRAYER. *May I seek You, Lord, by praying to You, and let me pray to You by believing in You. You have been preached to us. My faith prays to You, Lord, the faith You gave me and inspired in me by the Incarnation of Your Son and the mission of Your preacher.* — *Confessions 1, 1*

JULY 20

Two Kinds of People

ESSENTIALLY, there are two kinds of people, because there are two kinds of love. One is holy the other is selfish. One is subject to God; the other endeavors to equal Him.

One is friendly; the other is envious. One wishes for the neighbor what it would wish for itself; the other wishes to subject the neighbor to itself. One guides the neighbor in the interests of the neighbor's good; the other guides the neighbor for its own interests.

— *The Literal Meaning of Genesis 11, 15*

PRAYER. *Lord, You are delightful food for the pure of heart.* — *Confessions 13, 21*

JULY 21

The Devil's Entry: Cupidity and Fear

NOW the devil does not seduce or influence anyone unless he finds that person already somewhat similar to himself. He finds someone coveting something, and cupidity opens the door for the devil's suggestion to enter.

The devil finds someone fearing something, and he advises that person to flee what is feared. By these two doors, cupidity and fear, the devil gains entry. — *Sermon 12, 11*

PRAYER. *Lord, You have saved my soul from the constraint cf fear, so that it may serve You in the freedom of love.* — *Commentary on Psalm 30 (1), 8*

JULY 22

Our End

O UR prayer is "Make known to me, O Lord, my end." The end is where we are going to stay. When we left our houses, our end was to come to church. Again, from here each one of us has the end of going home. We end in the place we are going to.

So now here we all are, engaged in life's pilgrimage, and we have an end we are going toward. Toward what are we going? Toward our home country. What is our home country? Jerusalem, mother of the faithful, mother of the living! — *Sermon 16A, 9*

PRAYER. *You, the Omnipotent and the Good, care for each of us as if each was Your sole care, and for all as for one alone!* — *Confessions 3, 11*

JULY 23

Love, the Guardian of Virginity

H ENCE, it is God alone Who both gives virginity and protects it. And God is Love! Love, therefore, is the guardian of virginity, but humility is the dwelling-place of this guardian. He indeed dwells there Who said that the Holy Spirit rests on the humble, the peaceful, and the one who fears His words.

Humble spouses more easily follow the Lamb than proud virgins. — *Holy Virginity 51, 52*

PRAYER. *Walk along the path of sublimity with the feet of humility.* — *Holy Virginity 52, 53*

JULY 24
The Needs of the Church over Contemplation

F the Church should request your services, do not accede to this request out of a desire to get ahead, nor refuse it moved by pleasureful idleness. Obey God, rather, in simplicity of heart, submitting yourselves humbly to Him Who directs you.

Neither should you prefer your peaceful leisure to the needs of the Church. If there were no people to minister to her as she gave birth, not even you would have found a way to have been born.

— Letter 48, 2

PRAYER. *Lord, those are Your best servants who wish to shape their life on Your answers rather than shape your answers on their wishes.*

— Confessions 10, 26

JULY 25
My Purpose Is to Reach My God

ERVENTLY, I seek my God in the material things of heaven and earth, and I do not find Him. I seek the reality of Him in my own soul, and I do not find it. Yet I am determined to seek my God.

In my yearning to understand and look into the invisible things of God by means of created things, I pour out my soul within me. I have no other purpose henceforth but to reach my God.

— Commentary on Psalm 41, 8

PRAYER. *I call upon You, my God, my Mercy, my Creator. I had forgotten You, but You held me ever in Your sight.* *— Confessions 13, 1*

JULY 26

Hungry for God

DDITIONALY, I sought for something to love, for I was in love with love. There was a hunger within me from a lack of inner food, which is none other than Yourself, my God. Yet that hunger did not make me hungry.

I had no desire for incorruptible food. This was not because I was already filled with it but because the more I was empty of it the more it was loathsome to me. — *Confessions 3, 1*

PRAYER. *O God, be my inheritance; I love You totally. With all my heart, with all my mind I love You.* — *Sermons 334, 3*

JULY 27

Two Cities

HERE are two cities, the city of the godly and the city of the ungodly. These have been with us since the human race began, and they will continue till the end of the world.

For the time being, as far as outward appearances go, they are indistinguishable, but their aspirations are very different. On the Day of Judgment they will be separated bodily for all to see. — *Catechetical Instructions 31*

PRAYER. *O God my Father, I am seeking You, not making statements about You. Help me and guide me.* — *Confessions 9, 17*

JULY 28
Love Reaches Out

OREOVER, this is the rule of love: the good that we desire for ourselves we desire for our neighbor also; and the evil that we are unwilling to undergo we wish to prevent from happening to our neighbor.

All who love God will have such a desire toward everybody.

— True Religion 87

PRAYER. *O Lord, my God, let my soul praise You that it may love You. Let it recount to You Your mercies that it may praise You for them all.*

— Confessions 5, 1

JULY 29
Chaste Fear

JUST from the fact that you try to avoid evil, you improve yourself, and you begin to desire what is good. When you begin to desire what is good, there will be a chaste fear in you.

That fear by which you fear being cast into hell with the devil is not yet chaste, since it does not come from the love of God but from fear of punishment. But when you fear God in the sense that you do not wish to lose Him, you embrace Him, and you desire to enjoy Him.

— Sermon on 1 John 9, 5

PRAYER. *Lord, I now love You alone, I follow You alone, and I seek You alone. I yearn to be possessed by You.* *— Soliloquies 1,1*

JULY 30

The Common Store

E lived in the bishop's house like those spoken of in the Acts of the Apostles: No one possessed anything personally, but they had all things in common.

We sold our possessions and gave to the poor, so that we would live from the common store. And common to all of us would be the exceedingly great property, God Himself.　— *Sermon 355, 2*

PRAYER. *Lord, whatever You give me is too little for me. Be Yourself my inheritance! I love You without reserve: with all my heart and all my soul and all my mind. Of what value is anything You give me that is not Yourself?* — *Sermon 334, 3*

JULY 31

Living in Unity

ROTHERS and sisters dwell together in unity not by their own strength or their own merits but by God's grace, like dew from heaven.

This dew comes from Christ. All you who wish to dwell in unity, desire this dew and be moistened by it. Otherwise you cannot hold firm what you profess.　— *Commentary on Psalm 132, 10-11*

PRAYER. *Lord, You are my helper and the helper of anyone who reaches out to You. Indeed, You are my Redeemer for the very purpose of enabling me to reach out to You*

— *Commentary on Psalm 18, 15*

AUGUST 1
The Healing Physician

BE assured that all your diseases will be healed. Have no fear. You may say that your diseases are powerful; but this physician is more powerful. There is no disease that the Almighty Physician cannot cure.

Just allow yourself to be healed and do not reject His healing hands. He knows what He is doing. — *Commentary on Psalm 72, 32*

PRAYER. Bring relief to a serious wound with Your great medicine. Mine is serious, but I take refuge in the Almighty. I would despair of such a grave injury unless I had recourse to a great physician. — *Commentary on Psalm 50, 6*

AUGUST 2
Lift Up Your Hearts

PUT the things of creation in the second place. You have to leave this world at some day, for you are not going to remain here forever. Each day you hear, "Lift up your hearts." But you sink your heart into this world as though you heard the very opposite.

Listen to me, you who are poor: what is lacking to you if you have God? Listen to me, you who are rich: what do you possess if you do not have God? — *Sermon 311, 14-15*

PRAYER. Lord, help us, so that a change may be achieved in us, and we may find You ready to offer Yourself for the enjoyment of those who love You. — *Commentary on Psalm 6, 5*

AUGUST 3
Temperance

ALL who love the world dwell in it by their love, just as all whose hearts are lifted upward dwell by their love in heaven. When we are commanded not to love the world, it does not mean we should refrain from eating, drinking, or begetting children.

But temperance is ordered because of the Creator, so that such things will not enslave you by your love of them. — *Sermon on 1 John 2, 12*

PRAYER. Command, Lord, and requisition whatever You wish. But heal and open my ears so that I may hear Your voice. Heal and open my eyes, so that I see You commanding. Drive the madness out of me, so that I may recognize myself. — *Soliloquies 1, 5*

AUGUST 4
Not Every Sin Is Sinful

MANY sins are committed through pride, but not all happen proudly. They happen so often out of ignorance and out of human weakness.

Many sins are even committed by people weeping and groaning in their distress.

— *Nature and Grace 29, 33*

PRAYER. Lord, I have done much wrong. I cannot hope for a speedy rest for myself. May my torments be enough till Your coming. Let me be tortured now. Then, when You come, spare me.

— *Sermon 327, 2*

AUGUST 5

A Redeemer Fashioned for Us

OD the Father said: "I sent you One Who would seek you out, walk with you, and forgive you. So He had feet to walk with and hands to forgive with.

Thus, when He ascended after His Resurrection, He showed hands, side, and feet: hands with which He gave pardon to sinners; and side from which flowed the ransom of the redeemed."

— Sermon 16A, 10

PRAYER. Come, Lord, and act. Rouse and renew us, kindle us and carry us away, shine before us and be gentle with us, let us love and run toward You. — Confessions 8, 4

AUGUST 6

You Are a Beggar of God

VEN though you possess plenty, you are still indigent. You abound in temporal possessions, but you need things eternal. You listen to the needs of a human beggar, yet you yourself are a beggar of God.

What you do with those who beg from you is what God will do with His beggar. You are filled and you are empty. Fill your empty neighbor from your fullness, so that your emptiness may be filled from God's fullness. — Sermon 56, 9

PRAYER. Lord, I have waited for You to come and deliver me from every need. For in my need You have not forsaken Your law of mercy.

— Commentary on Psalm 129, 3

AUGUST 7
You Must Be Drawn

UR Lord said: "No one can come to Me unless the Father Who sent Me draws that person." This is a great commendation of grace!

Do not make judgments about whom God draws and whom He does not draw, unless you wish to fall into error. Accept this once and for all, and understand it: you are not yet drawn to God? Pray that you may be drawn!

— *Sermon on John 26, 2*

PRAYER. *Lord, heal and open my eyes that I may recognize Your will. Put to flight my foolishness that I may know You. Show me the road I must travel that I may see You. Thus aided, I hope to do all You have commanded me.* — *Soliloquies 1, 5*

AUGUST 8
Prayer and Temptation

ITHOUT doubt, we must pray lest we enter into temptation. This is denied by those who claim that God's aid is not necessary for humankind to keep free from sin and that the human will that merely knows the law is sufficient.

Such persons should certainly be kept out of the hearing of everyone and should be rejected by the unanimous voice of all. — *Human Justice, 44*

PRAYER. *Lord Jesus, You suffered for us not for Yourself. You bore the punishment for no fault of Your own, to abolish both the fault and the punishment.* — *Sermon 136, 6*

AUGUST 9
Christ's Members Follow the Head

YOU must realize that when the Father shows His works to Christ's members, it is to Christ that He shows them. He shows them to the members through the Head.

Suppose you wish to take hold of some object with your eyes closed. Your hand does not know where to go, yet your hand is your member. Open your eyes. and your hand will now see where it must go. The member follows the way indicated by its head! — *Sermon on John 21, 9*

PRAYER. *Lord, only this do I ask of Your great kindness: that You convert me totally to You and allow no obstacle to hinder me as I wend my way to You.* — *Soliloquies 1, 6*

AUGUST 10
Let Friends Help Us

FOR when we are harassed by poverty, saddened by bereavement, ill, or in pain, let good friends visit us. Let them be persons who not only can rejoice with those who rejoice but can weep with those who weep.

Let them be persons who know how to give useful advice and how to win us to express our own feelings in conversation. — *Letter 130, 2*

PRAYER. *O Lord, my God, pay heed to my prayer. Look with mercy on my desire, which is not concerned with myself alone but with my neighbor's good as well.* — *Confessions 11, 2*

AUGUST 11
Two Types of Fear

SHALL I say something about the two types of fear? There is a servile fear and there is a chaste fear. The first fears that it may suffer punishment; the other fears that it may lose justice.

The chaste fear endures forever. Love does not destroy it or drive it out of us, but rather embraces it and holds on to it as its companion. We come to the Lord in order to see Him face to face. Then a chaste fear preserves us.

— *Sermon on John 43, 7*

PRAYER. *I implore You, God, You to Whom faith calls us, hope leads us, and love unites us. Come to me in Your mercy.* — *Soliloquies 1, 3*

AUGUST 12
You Loved Me First

LOOK down upon me and have mercy on me according to the judgment of those who love Your Name. For You first loved me, so that I might love You. By loving You, I love myself, and thus I am wisely able also to love my neighbor as myself.

Lord, teach me how to act; teach me how to do Your will. For though I hear, and bear in mind what I hear, I am by no means supposed to have learned if I do not act.

— *Commentary on Psalm 118 (27), 5-8*

PRAYER. *Lord, You first loved me, so that I might love You.* — *Commentary on Psalm 118 (27), 15*

AUGUST 13

Rich and Poor—Equal Births

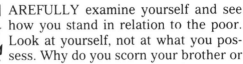 AREFULLY examine yourself and see how you stand in relation to the poor. Look at yourself, not at what you possess. Why do you scorn your brother or sister? In your mother's wombs both of you were naked. In truth, even when you have departed this life, and your bodies have rotted, when your souls have been sent forth, can the bones of the rich and poor people be told apart?

I am speaking of the condition of humankind in which all are born. For both things are true: a person becomes rich here and a poor person will not be here forever.   — *Commentary on Psalm 103, 7*

PRAYER. *God examines rich and poor, not according to their lands and houses, but according to the riches of their hearts.*

— *Commentary on Psalm 48, 3*

AUGUST 14

Death Starts with Life

EST assured that the possibility of death starts with the beginning of life. In this world of ours, only those who are not yet born can claim not to be as yet due to die.

That is why the uncertain day of death becomes a daily contingence for you and me alike.

— *Sermon 9, 2*

PRAYER. *Eternal Truth, true Love, beloved Trinity—all this, my God, You are, and it is to You that I sigh by night and by day.* — *Confessions 7, 10*

AUGUST 15

Mary and the Church

ARY gave birth to your Head, and the Church gave birth to you. For the Church also is both mother and virgin. She is mother by her entrails of charity, and virgin by the integrity of faith and piety.

She gives birth to many, but they are all members of One whose Body and spouse she herself is. In this she is like Mary, because in many she is the mother of unity. — *Sermon 192, 2*

PRAYER. Come, let us adore Him Whom the Virgin conceived without concupiscence, to Whom she gave birth as a virgin and remained thereafter a virgin. — *Sermon 231, 2*

AUGUST 16

The Beauty of Singing

INDEED, Lord, the days were not long enough as I found wonderful delight in meditating upon the depth of Your design for the salvation of the human race. I wept at the beauty of Your hymns, and I was powerfully moved at the sweet sound of Your Church's singing.

Those sounds flowed into my ears, and the truth streamed into my heart. My feeling of devotion overflowed, and the tears ran from my eyes, and I was happy in them. — *Confessions 9, 6*

PRAYER. O Lord, my God, let my soul praise You that it may love You. Let it recount to You Your mercies that it may praise You for them all.
— *Confessions 5, 1*

AUGUST 17

The Force of Habit

NDENIABLY, we have the free power to do or not to do anything, before we are caught up in any habit. When we have used this freedom to do something, the sweetness and pleasure of the act holds our soul, and it is caught up in the sort of habit that it cannot break—by its own act of sin.

If you want to see what I mean, start trying not to swear: then you will see how the force of habit goes its own way. — *Against Fortunatus 22*

PRAYER. *Lord, You are never needy, yet You are pleased with gain. You are never covetous, yet You exact interest on all You give us.*
— *Confessions 1, 4*

AUGUST 18

Perseverance into Old Age

PLEASE forgive me if I have spoken too much. I am a long-winded old man, and ill health has made me anxious. As you see, I have grown old with the passing years. But for a long time now, this ill health has made an old man of me.

However, if God is pleased with what I have just said, He will give me strength. I will not desert you. — *Sermon 355, 7*

PRAYER. *Lord, with Your help we have done what You commanded. Reward us, now, as You promised.*
— *Seremon 31, 6*

AUGUST 19

The Providence of God

GOD is the unchanging conductor as well as the unchanged creator of all things that change. When He adds, abolishes, curtails, increases, or diminishes the rites of any age, He is ordering all events according to His providence.

This will hold good until the beauty of the completed course of time—whose parts are the dispensations suitable to each different period—shall have played itself out, like the great melody of some ineffable composer. — *Letter 138, 1*

PRAYER. *Instruct me, Lord, and command what You will. But first heal me and open my ears that I may hear Your words.* — *Soliloquies 1, 1*

AUGUST 20

Legitimate Human Longing

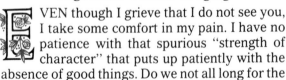EVEN though I grieve that I do not see you, I take some comfort in my pain. I have no patience with that spurious "strength of character" that puts up patiently with the absence of good things. Do we not all long for the future Jerusalem?

I cannot refrain from this longing; I would be inhuman if I could. Indeed, I derive some sweetness from my very lack of self-control. And in this sweet yearning I seek some small consolation. — *Letter 27, 1*

PRAYER. *Lord, show me the way I must travel that I may see You.* — *Soliloquies 1, 1*

AUGUST 21
Absence of Friends

ONE day, you yourself will begin to have to surrender some of the very dearest of those you have reared, to the needs of churches situated far from you.

It is then that you will understand the pangs of longing that stab me on losing the physical presence of friends united to me in the most close and sweet intimacy.

— *Letter 84, 1*

PRAYER. *As long as we are here, let us ask God not to deprive us of our prayer and His mercy, so that we may pray with perseverance and He may have mercy with His perseverance.*

— *Commentary on Psalm 65, 24*

AUGUST 22
Sing with Human Reason

DEAR friends, sing the Psalm with human reason, not like birds. Thrushes, parrots, ravens, magpies, and the like are often taught to say what they do not understand. However, to know what we are saying was granted by God's will to human nature.

Hence, we who have learned in the Church to sing God's words should be eager to do so. We should know and see with a clear mind what we have all sung together with one voice.

— *Commentary on Psalm 18, 2*

PRAYER. *Give me strength to seek You, Lord, for You have already enabled me to find You and have given me hope of finding You ever more fully.*

— *The Trinity 15, 51*

AUGUST 23
Talents Are for Others

JESUS said: "To the person who has, it shall be given." God will give more to those who use for others that which they have received. He will fill up and pile to the brim what He first gave.

Our reflections will be multiplied at His prompting. Thus, in our service of Him we will suffer no shortage but will rather rejoice in a miraculous abundance of ideas.

— *Christian Doctrine, 1, 1*

PRAYER. *Lord, my knowledge and my ignorance lie before You. Where You have opened to me, let me enter. Where You have closed to me, open when I knock* — *The Trinity, 15, 51*

AUGUST 24
Praying for Others

LET me be helped by your prayers, so that the Lord may see fit to help me bear His burden. When you pray in this way, it is really for yourselves that you are praying. For what is the burden of which I am speaking but you?

Pray for me, then, as I myself pray that you may not be burdensome. Support me so that we may bear one another's burdens, thus fulfilling the law of Christ. — *Sermon 340, 1*

PRAYER. *Lord, those who are bowed down with burdens You lift up, and they do not fall because You are their support.* — *Confessions 11, 31*

AUGUST 25

Vocations in a Monastery

ALTHOUGH good order reigns in my household, I am human and I live among humans. I would not dare to say that my home is better than the community of the Lord Christ, in which eleven faithful souls put up with the faithless thief Judas.

Yet with great difficulty have I met persons better than those who have made progress in the monastery. — *Letter 78, 8-9*

PRAYER. *Thanks be to Him Who is desired before He is seen, whose presence is felt, and Who is hoped for in the future.* — *Sermon 24, 1*

AUGUST 26

The Inner Voice

CONSIDER this great mystery. The sound of my words strikes the ears, and the Master is within! Do not suppose that any human is the teacher of another. We can admonish by the sound of our voice; but unless there is one Who teaches on the inside, the sound we make is futile.

I, for my part, have spoken to all; but those to whom the Anointing within does not speak, those whom the Holy Spirit within does not teach, go back untaught. — *Sermon on 1 John 3, 12*

PRAYER. *Instruct me, Lord, and command what You will. But first heal me and open my ears that I may hear Your words.* — *Soliloquies 1, 5*

AUGUST 27
Caught Up in Ecstasy

NOW, while my mother and I were thus talking of God's wisdom and pining for it, with all the effort of our hearts we did for one instant attain to touch it. Then we returned to the sound of our own tongue, in which words must have a beginning and an end.

We said: If in the silence of all earthly things God alone spoke to us, not by them but by Himself, would not this constitute to "enter into the joy of the Master"? — *Confessions 9, 10*

PRAYER. *Lord, let those who understand, praise You. And let those who understand You not, praise You too.* — *Confessions 11, 31*

AUGUST 28
For You I Am the Bishop

BELIEVE me, brothers and sisters, if what I am for you frightens me, what I am with you reassures me. For you I am the bishop; with you I am a Christian.

"Bishop," this is the title of an office one has accepted to discharge; "Christian," that is the name of the grace one receives. Dangerous title! Salutary name! — *Sermon 340, 1*

PRAYER. *Lord, whether prosperity smiles or adversity frowns, let Your praise be ever in my mouth.* — *Commentary on Psalm 138, 16*

AUGUST 29
Love—the Distinguishing Sign

OVE is the only sign that distinguishes the children of God from the children of the devil. To prove this, let them all sign themselves with the cross of Christ. Let them all respond: Amen. Let all sing: Alleluia. Let all build the walls of churches.

There is still no way of discerning the children of God from the children of the devil except by love! — *Sermon on 1 John 5, 7*

PRAYER. *Come to my aid, O God, the one eternal, true reality! In You there is no strife, no disorder, no change, no need, no death, but supreme harmony, supreme clarity, supreme permanence, supreme life.* — *Soliloquies 1, 1*

AUGUST 30
Every Moment You Are Passing On

ROM the time that I started speaking until this moment, do you realize you have grown older? You cannot see your hair growing. Yet while you stand around, while you are here, while you do something, while you talk, your hair keeps on growing—but never so suddenly that you need a barber straightaway

In this way, your existence fades away. You are passing on. — *Commentary on Psalm 38, 12*

PRAYER. *My God, let me be thankful as I remember and acknowledge all Your mercies.*

129

— *Confessions 8, 1*

AUGUST 31
Light to My Lamp

REMEMBER, even those who live justly do so not through human merits but through divine helps. No persons live justly unless they have been made just; and humans are made just by Him Who can never be unjust.

As a lamp is not lighted by itself, so the human soul does not give light to itself but calls out to God: "You indeed, O Lord, give light to my lamp." — *Commentary on Psalm 110, 2*

PRAYER. *You will light my lamp, Lord my God. I stand in the darkness of my sins, but my shadows will be dispelled by the beam of Your wisdom and Your face will shine upon me.*

— *Commentary on Psalm 66, 4*

SEPTEMBER 1
Christ Our Way

JESUS said: "I am the Way, the Truth, and the Life." He meant: It is by Me that you come; it is to Me that You come; and it is in Me that you remain. How do you wish to go? I am the Way. Where do you wish to go? I am the Truth. Where do you wish to remain? I am the Life.

Christ as God is the homeland where we are going. Christ as Man is the Way we must travel.

— *Christian Doctrine 1, 34*

PRAYER. *O Lord, my God, You alone do I love; You alone do I follow; You alone do I seek. You alone am I prepared to serve.* — *Soliloquies 1, 15*

SEPTEMBER 2

The Testimony of Creation

WHEN I asked the earth, it responded: "I am not God." When I asked the heavens, the sun, the moon, the stars, they said: "Nor are we the God you seek." I said: "Speak to me of my God."

Loudly, they exclaimed: "It is He Who made us." The heavens, the earth, and everything that is in them, all these things tell me to love You.

— *Confessions 10, 6*

PRAYER. *It was You, O Lord, Who created the heavens and earth. They are beautiful because You are beautiful. They are good because You are good. They have come to be because You are.* — *Confessions 11, 4*

SEPTEMBER 3

The Lord Is Within

YOU, Lord, were within me, while I was outside. It was there that I sought you. I rushed headlong upon these things of beauty that You had made.

You were with me, but I was not with You. They kept me far from You, those fair things which, if they were not in You, would not exist at all! — *Confessions 10, 27*

PRAYER. *Let me know You, my Father, let me know You as I too am known. Enter my soul, You Who are its strength, and make it what You want, so that You may have and possess it without stain or wrinkle.* — *Confessions 10, 1*

SEPTEMBER 4
Love of Neighbor

PERSONS who love God cannot despise Him when He commands us to love our neighbor. And do those who in spiritual holiness love their neighbor love anything but God in that neighbor?

Let us, then, love one another, so that, we may attract one another to love God in ourselves by means of love. In this way we may be closely united and be the Body of such a Head!

—*Sermon on John 65, 2*

PRAYER. *Increase my faith, Lord, increase my hope, and increase my love! How wonderful and unmatched is Your goodness!* — *Soliloquies 1, 1*

SEPTEMBER 5
The Lord Builds the House

UNLESS the Lord builds the house, the builders labor in vain, declares the Psalmist. Who are those who labor to build it? All those who in the Church preach the word of God, the ministers of God's Sacraments.

But "unless the Lord builds the house, the builders labor in vain." We speak from without; He builds from within. It is He Who builds, counsels, inspires fear, opens your minds and directs them to the faith. — *Commentary on Psalm 126, 1*

PRAYER. *Lord, I have asked for only one thing from You, to live in Your house all the days of my life, to gaze upon Your delight.*

— *Commentary on Psalm 26 (2), 17*

SEPTEMBER 6

O Beauty, So Ancient and So New

TOO late have I loved You, O Beauty so ancient and so new, too late have I loved You. You have called to me, and have cried out, and have shattered my deafness. You have blazed forth with light and have put my blindness to flight!

You have sent forth fragrance, and I have drawn in my breath, and I pant after You. I have tasted You, and I hunger and thirst after You. You have touched me, and I have burned for Your peace.
— Confessions 10, 27

PRAYER. *My faith, O Lord, which You gave me through the humanity of Your Son, calls upon You.*
— Confessions 1, 1

SEPTEMBER 7

Admiration for the Dedicated

HOW can we help but admire and commend those who disregard and set aside the pleasures of this world and live together in a truly chaste and holy society! They pass their time in prayers, readings, and discussions, without any swelling of pride, or noise of contention, or sullenness of envy.

Quiet, modest, and peaceful, their life is one of perfect harmony and devotion to God.
— The Morals of the Catholic Church 31, 67

PRAYER. *Give me Yourself, O my God. Surrender Yourself to me, for I love You. And if that is not enough, let me love You more ardently.*

— Confessions 13, 8

SEPTEMBER 8

Mary and the Church

MARY is holy; she is blessed. Yet the Church is better than the Virgin Mary. Why? Because Mary is a part of the Church, a holy member, an excellent member, of the Body.

If Mary is a part of the whole Body, it is clear that the Body is greater than its mother.

— *Sermon 72A, 7*

PRAYER. *Let our beautiful God, the Word with God, come to us that we may gaze upon Him with the eyes of our minds. He was beautiful in the womb of the Virgin where, in taking on our humanity, He nonetheless did not lose His divinity.* — *Commentary on Psalm 44, 3*

SEPTEMBER 9

Christ Is Needy in His Followers

ACCORDINGLY, when Christian receives Christian, the members serve one another; and the Head rejoices and considers given to Himself what was bestowed on His member.

On our journey, we must live where Christ is in need. He is needy in His followers, for He Himself has no needs. — *Sermon 236, 3*

PRAYER. *Lord, You perfected my love so that I might surmount the dark entanglements of this world. Direct my desire toward the heavenly home so that I may be enriched with every good thing.* — *Commentary on Psalm 17, 34*

SEPTEMBER 10

The One Vow All Must Make

D O not make vows and then neglect to keep them. What vow are we all expected to make without distinction? The vow of believing in Christ, hoping for eternal life from Him and living a good life in keeping with the ordinary norms of good conduct.

As for any other vows, let each of us make any we wish. But let us also take care to observe the ones we have made! — *Commentary on Psalm 75, 16*

PRAYER. *Lord, all that I am I am with Your mercy.*
— *Sermon 16A, 6*

SEPTEMBER 11

The Way of Correction

B E assured that abuses are not done away with by harsh or severe or autocratic measures, but by teaching rather than by commanding, by persuasion rather than by threats. This is the way to deal with the people in general, reserving severity for the sins of the few.

If we make threats, let it be done sorrowfuly, in the words of Scripture, and in terms of the world to come. In this way, it is not we who are feared because of our power, but God because of our words.
— *Letter 22, 5*

PRAYER. *Thanks and praise to You, my God, Who sound in my ears and illuminate my heart. Keep me away from every temptation.*
— *Confessions 10, 31*

SEPTEMBER 12

Love the Creator in the Creature

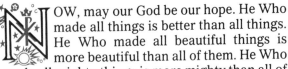OW, may our God be our hope. He Who made all things is better than all things. He Who made all beautiful things is more beautiful than all of them. He Who made all mighty things is more mighty than all of them. He Who made all great things is greater than all of them.

Learn to love the Creator in His creature, and the maker in what He has made.

— *Commentary on Psalm 39, 9*

PRAYER. *O Lord, my God, You alone do I love; You alone do I follow; You alone do I seek. You alone am I prepared to serve, for You alone justly rule, and under Your authority I long to be.*

— *Soliloquies 1, 1*

SEPTEMBER 13

Charity Constitutes Your Roots

ATCH the tree. First it seeks the depths in order to grow high. It drives roots into the depths so that it can raise its top toward the sky. Does it have any other foundation than lowness?

In the light of this, do you wish to attain to the heights without charity? Without roots do you seek the upper airs? — *Sermon 117, 17*

PRAYER. *Alas for me, O Lord, how high You are in the heights, and how deep in the depths! Nowhere do You withdraw, yet we scarcely return to You!*

— *Confessions 8, 3*

SEPTEMBER 14

Mystery of the Wooden Cross

NOW this: just as the wood of the ark saved the just from drowning, so too, by the mystery of His wooden Cross, does Christ, the Church's God and King, save us from drowning in the sea of this world.

In the symbol of a thing made of wood He gave human beings a foreshadowing of both the judgment to come and the salvation of the just.

— *Catechetical Instructions 31*

PRAYER. *Lord, You help those who turn to You. Redeem us so that we may come to You.*

— *Commentary on Psalm 17, 15*

SEPTEMBER 15

Pride—Beginning of an Evil will

PEOPLE would not have performed an evil work unless an evil will had preceded it. Now what else than pride could be the beginning of an evil will? What is pride but the desire of a height out of proportion to our state?

It is a height out of proportion to our state to leave God to Whom the soul should cling as its basis and to become in some way our own basis. This is what happens when the soul is too pleased with itself. — *City of God 14, 4*

PRAYER. *What shall I ask of You, kind Jesus? Through You all things were made, Son of God, yet You are made among all things, Son of Man. Why should we come and learn from You? "Because I am meek and humble of Heart."*

— *Holy Virginity 35*

SEPTEMBER 16
You Are a Work of God

IF you praise the works of God, then you will also have to praise yourself, for you too are a work of God. Here is how you can praise yourself yet not be proud. Praise not yourself but God in you.

Offer praise, not because you are this or that kind of person, but because God made you; not because you are capable of doing this or that, but because He works in you and through you.

— *Commentary on Psalm 144, 7*

PRAYER. *Behold, O Lord, we are Your little flock; we belong to You.* — *Confessions 10, 36*

SEPTEMBER 17
One Goal

WE know we are traveling together. If our pace is slow, go on ahead of us. We won't envy you but rather will seek to catch up with you. However, if you consider us capable of a quicker pace, run along with us.

There is only one goal, and we are all anxious to reach it—some at a slow pace and others at a fast pace. — *Sermon on a New Canticle 4, 4*

PRAYER. *Let everyone's sighs be uttered in longing for Christ. He should be the object of our desire since He, the all-beautiful One, loves repulsive people so that He might make them beautiful. Let us run to Him and cry out for Him.*

— *Sermon on John 10, 13*

SEPTEMBER 18

Removal of Social Evils by Education

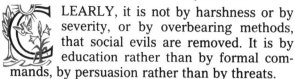 LEARLY, it is not by harshness or by severity, or by overbearing methods, that social evils are removed. It is by education rather than by formal commands, by persuasion rather than by threats.

This is the way to deal with people in general. Severity, however, should be employed only against the sins of the few. — *Letter 22, 5*

PRAYER. *Lord, You are the light of my heart and the bread in the mouth of my soul. You are the virtue dwelling in my mind and the hiding place of my thoughts.* — *Confessions 1, 13*

SEPTEMBER 19

True Superiors

UPERIORS are designated for the purpose of looking out for the good of their subjects. Hence, in the fulfillment of their office they should seek not their own advantage but that of their subjects.

There are superiors who delight in being placed over others, seek their own honor, and look out only for their own convenience. These are fattening themselves, not their flocks!

— *Sermon 46, 1*

PRAYER. *Lord, my own wrongdoing befouls me, and the offenses of others afflict me. Free me from theirs, and pardon me for mine. Take evil thoughts away from my heart, and keep me away from advisers of malice.*

— *Commentary on Psalm 18 (2), 13*

SEPTEMBER 20
Love for Sinners

 SSENTIALLY, the distinguishing mark of those who strive after Christian perfection is that they love the sinner and detest only sins.

When they must avenge wrongdoing, they do so, not with the cruelty of hatred, but with justice administered with moderation, lest forgiveness without satisfaction do more harm to the sinner than punishment. — *Against Adimantus 17*

PRAYER. *Lord, if the persecution of this world rises up against me, let me fix my hope on the prayer in my heart.* — *Commentary on Psalm 16, 3*

SEPTEMBER 21
The Fast and the Slow

ET those who are quicker than others in understanding reflect that they are walking along the road together with those who are slower. When one is faster than a companion, it is in the power of the faster to allow the slower to catch up, not vice versa.

If the faster walks with all possible speed, the slower will not succeed in following. The faster must slow the pace so as not to abandon the slower companion. — *Commentary on Psalm 90 (2), 1*

PRAYER. *I want to live in the house of the Lord all the days of my life. In it lies something wonderful to see, the delight of the Lord Himself awaiting our contemplation.*

— *Commentary on Psalm 26 (2), 8*

SEPTEMBER 22
We All Have One Teacher

REMEMBERING and bearing in mind the obligations of my servantship—such is my attitude as I teach you. Hence, I speak not as a master but as a minister, not to pupils but to fellow pupils since I speak not to servants but to fellow servants.

We all have one Master, whose school is on earth and whose seat is in heaven.

— *Sermon 242, 1*

PRAYER. *To those who love You, O Lord, according to Your command, You show Yourself, and it is enough for them. Thus they do not fall away from You nor back into themselves. This is the house of God, made not of the earth, nor of any physical heavenly body, but it is a spiritual sharing in Your eternity.* — *Confessions 12, 15*

SEPTEMBER 23
Renewal in Christ

OLD age has its many complaints: coughing, shaking, failing eyesight, anxiety, and weariness. The world is old, and it too is full of pressing tribulations.

Do not refuse to regain your youth in Christ Who says: The world is passing away. Do not fear. Your youth shall be renewed. — *Sermon 81, 8*

PRAYER. *You, O Lord, who always are, both before we were and before the world was, have become a refuge for us, within which we turn to You.* — *Commentary on Psalm 89, 3*

SEPTEMBER 24

Putting a Vocation to the Test

OW will you get to know the ones you want to exclude from the monastery? If you want to find out that they are unfit, you must put them to the test.

Many have promised themselves that they will generously respond to the holiness of that life. They have been put in the fire, and they have crumbled. — *Commentary on Psalm 99, 11*

PRAYER. *Lord, be my helper, and do not abandon me. See, I am on Your path. I have asked for only one thing from You, to live in Your house all the days of my life* — *Commentary on Psalm 26 (2), 17*

SEPTEMBER 25

The Grace of God

O one of us does anything good unless aided by Christ's grace. What we do badly comes from ourselves; what we do well, we do with the help of God.

Therefore, let us give thanks to God Who made it possible. And when we do well, let us not insult anyone who does not act in the same way. Let us not extol ourselves above such a person.

— *Commentary on Psalm 93, 15*

PRAYER. *Lord, I have seen Christ the Bridegroom. Let no one now lure me away from among the members of Your Bride. Be not my Head if I fail to be among her members.*

— *Commentary on Psalm 147, 18*

SEPTEMBER 26
You Owe Love

PRAYER is greatly aided by fasting and watching and every kind of bodily chastisement. In this regard each of you must do what you can.

Thus, the weaker will not hold back the stronger, and the stronger will not press the weaker. You owe your conscience to God. But to no one else do you owe anything more except that you love one another. — *Letter 130, 16*

PRAYER. Let me know You, O You Who know me. Let me know You just as I am known to You. Virtue of my soul, come into it and make it over for Your own use, that You may possess it without spot. — *Confessions 10, 1*

SEPTEMBER 27
Praying for Bodily Health

UNDOUBTEDLY, it is good that you request bodily health from God. If He knows that it is for your greater good, He will give it to you. If He does not give it, then it was not for your advantage.

God knows, therefore, what is better for us. Let us seek only that our heart be free from sin.

— *Sermon on John 7, 12*

PRAYER. Be a protecting God for me. I will not be saved unless it is in You. Unless You were my rest, my sickness would not be healed.

— *Commentary on Psalm 70 (1), 5*

SEPTEMBER 28

God's Correction Is for Our Good

MANIFESTLY, it is not true that the screams of someone undergoing a painful operation should hold back the hand of the surgeon who is skillfully operating! Is the surgeon cruel for continuing in order to heal the patient?

Seek nothing but God's help whenever you are corrected by Him. See to it that you do not perish, that you do not depart from the Lamb and be devoured by the lion! — *Sermon on John 7, 12*

PRAYER. Lord, You are the virtue dwelling in my mind and the hiding place of my thoughts!

— *Confessions 1, 13*

SEPTEMBER 29

Helping the Needy

WALKING by faith, let us do good works. In these let there be a free love of God for His own sake and an active love for our neighbor.

For there is nothing we can do for God. But because we have something we can do for our neighbor, we shall by our good offices to the needy gain the favor of Him Who is the source of all abundance. Let us then do what we can for others; let us freely bestow upon the needy out of our abundance. — *Sermon 41, 9*

PRAYER. Keep your eyes fixed on the Lord Who guides you, and do not look back.

— *Commentary on Psalm 75, 16*

SEPTEMBER 30
Lead Us Not into Temptation

OME persons think we receive no divine aid to avoid sins, since free choice of the will has been granted to our nature. Hence, according to them, it is not necessary to pray that we may not enter into temptation.

Their opinion is a harmful error, contrary and prejudicial to our salvation, which is in Christ.

— *On Merit and Forgiveness 2*

PRAYER. *My faith, O Lord, which You gave me through the humanity of Your Son, calls upon You.* — *Confessions 1, 1*

OCTOBER 1
Possess Us

HE Church is the Body of Christ and His temple and house and state. So He Who is the Head of the Body dwells in this house, sanctifies this temple, and is King of this state. As the Church is all these, so too is Christ.

What then have we promised to God, except that we be God's temple? We can offer Him nothing that is more pleasing than to say to Him: "Possess us!" — *Commentary on Psalm 131, 3*

PRAYER. *I want to live in the house of the Lord all the days of my life. In it lies something wonderful to see, the delight of the Lord Himself, awaiting our contemplation.*

— *Commentary on Psalm 26 (2), 8*

OCTOBER 2
Seek the Lord Within

OTE the Psalmist's words: "I sought the Lord, and He answered me." Where did the Lord hear? Within. Where does He reply? Within. There you pray, there you are heard, and there you are made happy.

Therefore, enter your heart. Happy are those who delight to enter their hearts and find no evil.

— *Commentary on Psalm 33 (2), 8*

PRAYER. *Lord, You strengthened me because I took refuge in You; and I took refuge because You freed me.* — *Commentary on Psalm 17, 3*

OCTOBER 3
Silence

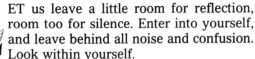ET us leave a little room for reflection, room too for silence. Enter into yourself, and leave behind all noise and confusion. Look within yourself.

See whether there be some delightful hidden place in your consciousness where you can be free of noise and argument, where you need not be carrying on your disputes and planning to have your own stubborn way. Hear the word in quietness, that you may understand it.

— *Sermon 52, 22*

PRAYER. *To those who love You, O Lord, according to Your command, You show Yourself, and it is enough for them. Thus they do not fall away from You nor back into themselves.*

— *Sermon 261, 1*

OCTOBER 4

Putting Up with Others

ALL who love their brothers and sisters put up with everything for the sake of unity, because neighborly love consists in the unity of love.

Suppose an evil person would offend you, or one whom you judge to be evil or even only imagine to be so. Would you, abandon so many others who are good? — *Sermon on 1 John 1, 12*

PRAYER. *You are all I possess, because You are my God. Shall I seek my father because of my inheritance? You, my God, are not only the giver of my inheritance but the inheritance itself!*

— *Commentary on Psalm 142, 17*

OCTOBER 5

Counterfeits in the Church

BROTHERS and sisters, allow no one to deceive you. If you do not wish to be deceived, and you want to love your brothers and sisters, then realize that every profession in the Church has its counterfeits.

I did not say that everyone is a counterfeit, but that every profession includes people who are counterfeit. There are bad Christians just as there are good ones. — *Commentary on Psalm 99, 13*

PRAYER. *You are one God, and You come to my aid. In You nothing is lacking and nothing is in excess. In You the One Who generates and the One generated are one alone.* — *Soliloquies 1, 4*

OCTOBER 6
Know Yourself

UNDERSTAND that no one is telling you: "Be less than you are"; but "know what you are." Know that you are human. Know that you are a sinner. Know that it is God Who frees you from blame.

Let your confession reveal the stain of your heart, and you will belong to the flock of Christ.

— *Sermon 137, 4*

PRAYER. *Lord, see Your work in me, not my own. For if You see my own work, You condemn me; but if You see Yours, You crown me. Whatever my good works are, they come from You and are therefore more Yours than mine.*

— *Commentary on Psalm 137, 18*

OCTOBER 7
Seriousness of Study

FOR my part, I prefer to do things in earnest, not to "play." If you chose the word to imply that what we do is easy, then let me tell you that I expected more of you.

It is your business to help those engaged in great and exacting investigations—as if studying the Scriptures were a matter of romping around on level ground, not puffing and panting up a steep mountainface. — *Letter 82, 1*

PRAYER. *Lord, because of Your Name may You have mercy on me according to Your great mercy, and by no means abandon the work You have begun but complete what is imperfect in me.* — *Confessions 10, 4*

OCTOBER 8
Strength in Christ

 NOW this: I have no fear of you. You cannot overturn the judgment seat of Christ and set up that of Donatus. I shall continue to call back the wandering; I shall seek out the lost.

Even if the branches of the wood tear me in my search, I shall still force my way through every path. Inasmuch as the Lord, Who drives me to this task by His terror, gives me strength, I shall go through everything. — *Sermon 46, 14*

PRAYER. *Lord our God, make us blessed by You, because we shall not lose You. When we remain true to You, we shall neither lose You nor be lost ourselves.* — *Sermon 113, 6*

OCTOBER 9
Truth Dwells Within

 O not go outside yourself but turn back within. Truth dwells in the inner self. And if you find your nature given to frequent change, go beyond yourself.

Move on, then, to that source where the light of reason itself receives its light.

— *True Religion 29, 72*

PRAYER. *I acknowledge You, O Lord, in Your humility, that I may not fear You in Your glory. I embrace You in Your lowliness. For to those who desire You, You come in clemency.*

— *Commentary on Psalm 66, 10*

OCTOBER 10

Our True Homeland

EXALTED is the homeland, and humble is the way. The homeland is the life of Christ, and His death is the way.

If anyone rejects the way, how can such a person seek the homeland?

— *Commentary on Psalm 28, 5*

PRAYER. *O Lord, I love You. I love, I burn, I pant for You; I trample under foot all that gives here delight. I want to go to You. Oh to love! Oh to go! Oh to die to myself! Oh to come to You!*

— *Sermon 159, 8*

OCTOBER 11

Embracing the Gospel

YOU must realize that I fondly love the perfection about which the Lord spoke when He said to the rich young man: "Go, sell all that you have and give to the poor, and you will have treasure in heaven, and come, follow Me." Not by my own strength, but with the aid of God's grace have I done this.

Persons who give up both what they possess and what they hope to possess give up the whole world. I encourage others to embrace this holy goal.

— *Letter 157, 39*

PRAYER. *Come, Lord, into my soul, which You have prepared for Your own reception by inspiring in me a longing for Your goodness.*

— *Confessions 13, 1*

OCTOBER 12

Living the Common Life

HERE in Hippo the clerics have decided with God's favor to follow the community form of life. Anyone who in the future is found to have his own possessions will not be allowed to dispose of them, and I will remove his name from the list of clerics.

I trust in God that as these men have accepted my arrangement with joy, so too they will keep it with purity and fidelity. — *Sermon 356, 14*

PRAYER. *Lord, I am poor and needy, and You are generous to all who appeal to You.*

— *Confessions 11, 2*

OCTOBER 13

Living Poverty

WHATEVER cleric wishes to dwell with me in voluntary poverty possesses God. If such a one is ready to be fed by God through his church, and to have nothing of his own, but rather to give what he has to the poor or to put it in the common store, let him remain with me.

If anyone does not wish this, he may have his freedom. But let him reflect whether he will have eternal happiness. — *Sermon 355, 6*

PRAYER. *Lord, I am poor and needy. I am better only when with heartfelt sorrow I renounce myself and seek Your mercy so that my deficiencies are overcome and transformed.*

— *Confessions 10, 38*

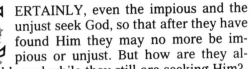

OCTOBER 14

Seek the Lord

CERTAINLY, even the impious and the unjust seek God, so that after they have found Him they may no more be impious or unjust. But how are they already blessed while they still are seeking Him?

They are happy by their hope not because of what they have but because of what they will have. They are happy, not because they seek God but because they will find what they seek.

— *Commentary on Psalm 138, 2-3*

PRAYER. O God, You are the Truth and the Light of my heart. Let me listen to You and not to the darkness within me. — *Confessions 12, 10*

OCTOBER 15

Brothers and Sisters at Peace

BAD brother or sister, quarrelsome brother or sister, you are still my brother or sister. You say, just as I say, "Our Father, Who art in heaven." Why, then, are we not together in one?

It is not a friend, not a neighbor, who orders us to be in harmony, but rather He to Whom we say, "Our Father." We have together one voice before our Father. Why do we not have one peace together? — *Sermon on John 26, 11*

PRAYER. Forgive us, Lord, all these things in which we have been led astray. Help us to resist being led away.

— *Punishment and the Forgiveness of Sins 2, 4*

OCTOBER 16
Bond of Fraternity

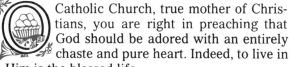 Catholic Church, true mother of Christians, you are right in preaching that God should be adored with an entirely chaste and pure heart. Indeed, to live in Him is the blessed life.

You also unite brothers and sisters to one another in a bond of religion that is stronger and closer than ties of blood. You unite citizen to citizen and people to people, not by a mere grouping together, but by the bond of fraternity.

— *The Customs of the Church 30, 62-63*

PRAYER. *O Sacrament of love, sign of our unity, bond of our fraternity, whoever long for life have here its very source. Let them come here and believe; unite with You and live.*

— *Sermon on John 26, 13*

OCTOBER 17
Praising God

OES not our mouth daily praise God as much as our limitations allow? What we praise is great, but the instrument by which we praise Him is still weak.

See how we stand and pray to God at some length. Our lips move often in song, but our thoughts rove about through all kinds of desires.

— *Commentary on Psalm 145, 6*

PRAYER. *The human person is one of Your creatures, Lord, and its instinct is to praise You.*

— *Confessions 1, 1*

OCTOBER 18
The Harbor of Life

REMOVED from the high waves of the outside world, those who have chosen a quiet life are, as it were, in a haven or a harbor. But where is their expected joy? They will still find causes for regret and problems with temptations.

Let us love one another. Let the ships in the harbor be carefully arranged with regard to one another, so that they not collide. Let the evenness of peers and a constant charity be observed there. — *Commentary on Psalm 99, 9*

PRAYER. *May God in His mercy grant that every day we may be troubled, tried, disciplined, or make some progress.* — *Sermon 16A, 12*

OCTOBER 19
Faith Working through Love

YOU have before you Christ as your end. You have no need to go on looking anymore. The moment you believed, you already recognized it.

But faith alone is not enough, unless works too are joined to it. "Faith working through love," says the Apostle! — *Sermon 16A, 11*

PRAYER. *Lord, my God, listen to my prayer, and may Your mercy hear my desire.*

— *Confessions 11, 2*

OCTOBER 20
Blessed the Peacemakers!

OME people are peacemakers in themselves. By conquering and subjecting to reason all the motions of their souls, and taming their carnal desires, they become, in themselves, a kingdom of God.

They enjoy the peace that is given on earth to persons of goodwill, the life of the consummate and perfect person of wisdom.

— Sermon on the Mount 1, 2

PRAYER. *Lord, whatever You give me is too little for me. Be You Yourself my inheritance! I love You with all my heart and all my soul and all my mind. Of what value is anything You give me that is not Yourself!* *— Sermon 334, 3*

OCTOBER 21
The Wedding Garment

OW what precisely is meant by the words, "My friend, how did you get in here without a wedding garment"? Listen to the Apostle: "If I give away all I have to the poor, if I hand over my body to be burnt, but have no love, it will avail me nothing."

So this is what the wedding garment is. Examine yourselves to see whether you possess it. If you do, your place at the Lord's table is secure. *— Sermon 90, 1. 6*

PRAYER. *O Lord, my God, let my soul praise You that it may love You. Let it recount to You Your mercies that it may praise You for them all.*

— Confessions 5, 1

OCTOBER 22
The Eternal Jerusalem

ORD, I will leave others outside, breathing into the dust and filling their eyes with earth. But I will enter into my room and sing my songs of love to You.

I will remember Jerusalem with my heart stretching upward in longing for it: Jerusalem my homeland, Jerusalem my mother!

— Confessions 12, 16

PRAYER. *You, O God, probe me and know me. You know that I do not give consent to the deeds of the wicked. Toward those who hate peace, I am peaceable, until I arrive at that vision understood to be Jerusalem, the mother of us all, the eternal city.* — Commentary on Psalm 138, 29

OCTOBER 23
Everyone Has Something To Give

RANKLY, even the poor have something they can share with others. Let one lend feet to the lame, another become the eyes of the blind, another visit the sick, and another bury the dead. These are things that everyone can do.

Lastly, bear one another's burdens, and so you shall fulfill the law of Christ. — *Sermon 41, 9*

PRAYER. *May He perfect His gifts in us, since He did not hesitate to take our faults on Himself. And may He make us children of God, since He chose to become the Child of humans for our sakes.* — Sermon 184, 3

OCTOBER 24
Beauty in Material Things

EAGERLY I sought to know how it was that I could appreciate beauty in material things and make correct judgments about things that are subject to change.

I realized that, above my changeable mind, there was the never-changing true eternity of truth. So, my mind attained to the sight of the God Who is. — *Confessions 7, 17*

PRAYER. *Look at the heavens and the earth: in their steady change and alteration they proclaim that they were made, and their very existence is itself the voice with which they speak. It was You, O Lord, Who created them.*

— *Confessions 11, 4*

OCTOBER 25
Youth to Old Age

UNQUESTIONABLY, in this life, we are all bound to die. Yet, as babies, we can look forward to childood; as children, to youth; and as youths, to adulthood.

As adults we can look forward to reaching our prime; and in our prime, to growing old. But the aged have no further stage of life to look forward to. — *Letter 213, 1*

PRAYER. *Lord, be our strong support from childhood to old age. For when our strength is Yours, then we are strong indeed. But when our strength is ours, we are feeble and weak.*

— *Confessions 4, 16*

OCTOBER 26

Pain for the Sake of Healing

GRATEFULLY will I receive a rebuke offered in such a friendly way. If I receive your correction calmly as a medicine, I shall not be pained by it—even though, because of a natural or personal weakness I cannot help feeling saddened.

Nonetheless, it is better to put up with the pain while the abscess is being healed, rather than not be cured so as to avoid the pain. — *Letter 73, 2*

PRAYER. *Lord, while I was still far away from You, You coaxed me in a great many ways to hear You from afar and be converted to You and call upon You.* — *Confessions 13, 1*

OCTOBER 27

The Object of Our Joy

JOY—who can live without it? Do you think that those who reverence, worship, and love God have no joys? Do you think that the arts and the theater, hunting and fowling and fishing all bring joy, but God's works do not?

Do you think that meditation on God does not bring its inner joys?

— *Commentary on Psalm 76, 14*

PRAYER. *O God, come to me in Your kindness. For You are the good and the beautiful, in Whom, by Whom, and through Whom all things are good and beautiful.* — *Soliloquies 1, 1*

OCTOBER 28

Let Them Live Well

ALL who eat the Lord's Flesh and drink His Blood must consider what they eat and drink. To avoid eating and drinking unto condemnation, let them live well.

You who are married, keep faithful to your partners. You who are not yet married, keep yourselves pure for your future spouses.

— Sermon 132, 1

PRAYER. *O Lord, I have passed on Your word. Now may You convert us to You; may You spare us. Make chaste those who have been unchaste, so that we all may rejoice in Your sight at the time of judgment.* — *Sermon 132, 1*

OCTOBER 29

The Proving of Christians

THE tempting of Christians is the proving of Christians. Either they are shown what they have or else they are shown what they lack.

Abraham was tempted, not for him to be shown what he didn't have, but for us to be shown what we should imitate. *— Sermon 16A, 12*

PRAYER. *You are the one God: come to me with Your aid. Under You the whole world keeps balance in the order and repetition of time: in the days, changing from daylight to night; in the months, with the waxing and waning of the moon; in the years with the passing of seasons.*

— Soliloquies 1, 1

159

OCTOBER 30

The Need for Daily Bread

WHEN you say; "Give us this day our daily bread," you admit that you are God's beggar. But do not be ashamed; however rich anyone may be on earth, that person is God's beggar. The beggar stands before the house of the rich Being.

Rich people need their "daily bread." Why do they have an abundance of everything? For no other reason than that God has given it to them. What, then, will they have if God should withdraw His aid? — *Sermon 56, 9*

PRAYER. Lord, all things are Yours, for You made them. We thank You. — *Sermon 16A, 6*

OCTOBER 31

Request the Gift of God Himself

CERTAINLY, God has given you much, but you have not yet received the robe of immortality. Why request no more as though you were filled to satiety?

If God is good to you because He has given you these things, how much more blessed will you be when He gives Himself to you! Request the gift of God Himself! — *Commentary on Psalm 144, 2*

PRAYER. I call upon You, my God, my Mercy, my Creator. I had forgotten You, but You held me ever in Your sight. Come, then, into my soul, which You have prepared for Your own reception by inspiring in me a longing for Your goodness. — *Confessions 13, 1*

NOVEMBER 1

The Holy Martyrs

T HOSE who spout vain words and are true Philistines do not form part of the family of Christ. "Who can equal me? Who dares attack me?" Is not this the language of those who pride themselves on their own resources? The just will bring low all that pride.

This is what martyrs did. They vanquished the wicked at the very moment when the latter appeared to be victorious. — *Sermon 32, 4*

PRAYER. *Lord, You are delightful food for the pure of heart.* — *Confessions 13, 21*

NOVEMBER 2

Good Life—Fearless Death

S CRIPTURE says: "Precious in the eyes of the Lord is the death of His holy ones." We must look upon the mystery of death with the eyes of faith so that we shall believe what we do not see and shall bear with fortitude the evils to which we are unjustly subjected.

Admittedly, it is not in our power to determine how our death may come about. However, it does lie in our power to determine how we live, so that we may die without fear. — *Sermon 306, 2*

PRAYER. *O death, when you seized my Lord, you then lost your grip on me.* — *Sermon 233, 5*

NOVEMBER 3
True Health in Immortality

FROM the time of our birth we are under the necessity of dying. "This sickness must end in death." So say the physicians when they examine the sick.

When therefore is true health found? Only when real immortality is reached. And there is no need for food there! So do not prepare your stomach but your spirit. — *Sermon 77, 14*

PRAYER. *Lord, You are our Physician, healing the ills of all. You reduce the swelling of pride, renew wasted life, and excise what is superfluous. You preserve what is necessary, restore what has been lost, and cure what has been corrupted.* — *Christian Combat, 11, 12*

NOVEMBER 4
Fear Everlasting Punishment

GOD has threatened evildoers with the burning fires of hell and everlasting flames. First compare these two things: death in a moment and punishments that last forever. You fear the former, but it will come whether you wish it or not.

You should rather fear everlasting punishment, which will not come to you if you do not wish. — *Sermon 279, 9*

PRAYER. *Remember me, O Lord, not according to Your wrath, but according to Your mercy. This befits You, O Lord, not owing to my merit but to Your kindness.* — *Commentary on Psalm 24, 7*

NOVEMBER 5

Choose Not To Die Forever

BVIOUSLY, you will not escape death, whether you live well or whether you live badly. But if you choose to live well in this life, you will not be cast into eternal punishments. So while you are still alive choose wisely not to die forever!

This is shown by Christ in His death and resurrection. By dying He showed what you are going to endure whether you wish to or not. But by rising from the dead, He showed what you also will receive if you lead a good life. — *Sermon 279, 9*

PRAYER. *O happy home! O land of safety! May I dwell there in security! From there I shall not seek to depart, for no safer place shall I find.*

— *Sermon 217, 2-3*

NOVEMBER 6

Brief Teaching

ERE is a brief teaching: you should realize that He gives with mercy when He gives and takes away with mercy when He takes away. Yet do not think that you are neglected by His mercy, since He either bolsters you through His gifts lest you weaken, or corrects you in your pride lest you perish. — *Commentary on Psalm 144, 4*

PRAYER. *Lord, You have become a refuge for us, that You might care for those who deserted You. You are a refuge so that you can encourage and guide Your children.* — *Sermon 55, 6*

NOVEMBER 7

Fear Only What You Can Avoid

COME now, are you going to avoid death if you do not wish to die? Why do you fear what you cannot avoid? You fear what is going to be even though you do not wish it—death. But you do not fear what will not be if you do not wish it—eternal punishment!

You cannot avoid death—you can merely postpone it. It will come even though you are unwilling.
— *Sermon 279, 9*

PRAYER. *O Lord, I ask you for instruction that through my trials I may learn what I should seek. I ask You then for eternal life. Please hear me: it is a place at Your right hand I seek.*

— *Commentary on Psalm 59, 1*

NOVEMBER 8

Strength in God's Grace

MY brothers and sisters, all our strength lies in the knowledge of God and the reception of His grace—in which David placed all his confidence.

Goliath, on the contrary, counted only on himself, on his own strength. Like all proud people, his pride showed itself in his face, and it was in his face that the stone cast by David struck him and felled him.
— *Sermon 32, 3*

PRAYER. *We did not exist when we were predestined, we were hostile when we were called, and we were sinners when we were justified. Then let us give thanks to God and not remain ungrateful.*

— *Sermon 158, 3*

164

NOVEMBER 9
We Are the Church

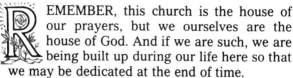 EMEMBER, this church is the house of our prayers, but we ourselves are the house of God. And if we are such, we are being built up during our life here so that we may be dedicated at the end of time.

A building, or rather the construction of that building, entails toil. The dedication, however, elicits only joy. But believers in Christ do not constitute a house of the Lord until they are joined together through love! *— Sermon 336, 1*

PRAYER. *Look, O Lord, upon the ranks of virgins and holy young men and women. Their kind has been brought up in Your Church.*

— Holy Virginity 36, 37

NOVEMBER 10
Warming the Cold One

ENCE, you who are fervent in spirit, be enkindled with the fire of love. Let your lives glow with the praises of God and irreproachable morals.

One person is hot, another cold. Let the one who is hot warm the cold. *— Sermon 234, 3*

PRAYER. *Glory to our Lord and to His mercy and to His truth! Out of His mercy He did not fail to make us blessed, nor did He hide from us His truth. The Truth, clad in flesh, came to us and healed through His flesh the inner eye of our heart, that afterward we might be able to see Him face to face. — Commentary on Psalm 56, 17*

NOVEMBER 11
The Miracle of Changes

BROTHERS and sisters, on this threshing floor grain can degenerate into chaff; and the chaff can be turned back into grain. These changes can take place daily.

This life is full of afflictions and consolations. Daily those who seemed good fall and perish; and again those who seemed evil are converted and live. — *Sermon 223, 2*

PRAYER. *I pray to You, God, Whom no one lets go, unless deceived; Whom no one seeks, unless taught; and Whom no one finds, unless cleansed. Come mercifully to me.* — *Soliloquies 1, 1*

NOVEMBER 12
Help the Incorrigible

UNDOUBTEDLY, it often happens that you try to correct certain depraved and dishonest people who are under your care, but every effort and concern is in vain. They are incorrigible, so they have to be put up with.

Such incorrigibles are already in the Church. How then will you separate yourself from them so that you are no longer burdened by them? Rather, be close to them: speak, exhort, coax, threaten, and correct them.

— *Commentary on Psalm 54, 8*

PRAYER. *Lord, hear my prayer, and let my soul not fail under Your protection.* — *Confessions 1, 15*

NOVEMBER 13

Final Goal

ILIGENTLY, our Lord manifested in His promises and prophecies the way in which we would arrive at our final goal. He promised human beings divinity, mortals immortality, sinners justification, and the poor a rising to glory.

Whatever He promised, He promised to those who were unworthy. Thus, it was not a case of a reward being promised to workers but of grace being given as a gift as its name indicates.

— Commentary on Psalm 110, 2

PRAYER. *Lord, my God, how great You are, and yet You make Your home in the humble of heart! It is You Who lift up the downtrodden, and You are their grandeur.* *— Confessions 11, 31*

NOVEMBER 14

Be Upright of Heart

F you want to be upright of heart, do not be displeased, over anything at all, with God.

If you see the reason for His doing what He does, do not find fault with Him. If the reason escapes you, understand that the thing is done by One with Whom it makes no sense at all to be displeased. *— Sermon 15A, 7*

PRAYER. *Blessed are those who love You, O God, and love their friends in You and their enemies for Your sake.* *— Confessions 4, 9*

NOVEMBER 15

Trust

A S you know, I have such a good opinion of my brothers that I have refrained from asking them questions. For it seemed to me that in questioning them I might almost appear to suspect some evil.

On the other hand, I was aware then as now that all those who have lived with me are familiar with our ideal and rule of life. — *Sermon 355, 2*

PRAYER. You, Lord, are the unfailing light, and from You I sought to know the existence, nature, and worth of all things, as I listened to Your teaching and commandments. — *Confessions 10, 40*

NOVEMBER 16

Dig Deep

L OOK, if you do not want to fear, probe your inmost self. Examine it with care. Does not a poisoned vein of the wasting love of the world still pulse there? Are you not moved by some physical desires or caught in some law of the senses? Are you never elated with empty boasting?

Only when you have sifted everything in the deepest recesses of your inner being can you dare to announce that you are pure and crystal clear. — *Sermon 348, 2*

PRAYER. Behold my heart, O Lord, my God. Look deep inside it and cleanse it of all disordered affection by directing my eyes to You and lifting my feet out of the snare. — *Confessions 4, 6*

NOVEMBER 17
Friendship Is Godlike

PARTICULARLY when I am worn out by the upsets of the world, I cast myself without reservation on the love of those who are especially close to me.

I know that I can safely entrust my thoughts and considerations to those who are aflame with Christian love and have become faithful friends to me. For I am entrusting them not to another human, but to God in Whom they dwell and by Whom they are who they are.   — *Letter 73, 3*

PRAYER. Lord, with Your help we have done what You commanded. Reward us as You promised.
                                        — *Sermon 31, 6*

NOVEMBER 18
A Rule of Life

HOLD dear the example of those who persevere and imitate it; weep for those who fall, lest you grow proud. Do not proclaim your righteousness but submit yourself to God Who frees you from blame.

Pardon the sins of others and pray for your own. Avoid future falls by vigilance and blot out past falls by confession.   — *Holy Virginity 52, 53*

PRAYER. Come, Lord, get to work on us. Call us back, kindle us, and clasp us to Your heart. Be fragrant to us all, and attract us by Your loveliness. Let us love You and run to You.

                                    — *Confessions 8, 4*

NOVEMBER 19

The City of God Sighs for Heaven

KNOW that the origin of the city of God goes back to Abel, as that of the evil one goes back to Cain. It is, therefore, an ancient city, this city of God: always enduring its existence on earth and always sighing for heaven. Its name is also Jerusalem and Zion.

— Commentary on Psalm 142, 2

PRAYER. *Lord, hear me and have mercy. Lord my God, You are the light of the blind and the strength of the weak, as well as the light of the sighted and the strength of the powerful. Attend to my soul, and hear the one crying from the depths.* — *Confessions 11, 2*

NOVEMBER 20

Captivity and Liberation

WE must also know first our captivity, then our liberation: we must know Babylon and Jerusalem. These were two cities recorded in the Bible.

They were founded to symbolize those two "cities" that began in the far past and will continue to the end of time.

— Commentary on Psalm 64, 1-2

PRAYER. *Lord, while I move and bear this body, I pray that I may be pure, generous, just, and prudent. May I be a perfect lover and knower of Your Wisdom. Finally, may I be worthy of Your Dwelling Place and live in Your most blessed Kingdom.* — *Soliloquies 1, 1*

NOVEMBER 21
Father and Judge

REALLY, what profit is there in temporal good health and in the ties of blood if we willingly spurn the eternal inheritance of Christ? And this opinion is not mine.

It comes from the words of Almighty God Himself: whoever rejects Him in this world as Father will find Him in the next as Judge! — *Letter 52, 4*

PRAYER. *O Lord, our God, let our mouths not speak of vanities. Make us happy in You, for we will not lose You if we have clung to You, nor shall we go lost. Make us happy in You.*

— *Sermon 113, 6*

NOVEMBER 22
Pine for the Homeland

NOW let us hear, brothers and sisters, let us hear and sing. Let us pine for the city where we are citizens. By pining, we are already there. We have already cast our hope, like an anchor, on that coast.

I sing of somewhere else, not of here; for I sing with my heart, not my flesh. The citizens of Babylon hear the sound of the flesh; the founder of Jerusalem hears the tune of the heart.

— *Commentary on Psalm 64, 3*

PRAYER. *Lord, let us make our home again in You and thus avoid being lost. Long ago we left it—for what is our home but Your Eternity, which does not disappear because we have deserted it!* — *Confessions 4, 16*

NOVEMBER 23

Christ Instructs Us in Silence

 NTER into your heart, as the Prophet Isaiah says. And, if you have faith, you will find Christ there. There He speaks to you.

I, the preacher, must raise my voice when I speak to you. But Christ instructs you more effectively in silence. — *Sermon 102, 2*

PRAYER. *O God, do not be silent to me, but speak the truth in my heart, for it is only truth You speak. Let me enter into the secret chamber of my heart and sing to You songs of love, which are largely sighs: my attempts to express what cannot be expressed.* — *Confessions 12, 16*

NOVEMBER 24

A Physician Who Does Not Charge

 OD sent the human race a physician, a savior, One Who healed without charging a fee. Christ also came to reward those who would be healed by Him.

Christ heals the sick, and He makes a gift to those whom He heals. And the gift that He makes is Himself! — *Sermon 156, 2*

PRAYER. *Lord, You are our Physician, healing the ills of all. You reduce the swelling of pride, renew wasted life, and excise what is superfluous. You preserve what is necessary, restore what has been lost, and cure what has been corrupted.* — *Christian Combat 11, 12*

NOVEMBER 25
Our Judge

B E assured that the One Who is now our defending lawyer will then be our judge. Can it be that we have Him as our defender and yet fear Him as our judge?

No! By the fact that, fully confident, we sent Him ahead to defend us, let us preserve our hope in Him when He comes to judge. — *Sermon 213, 5*

PRAYER. *It is You I desire, O Justice and Innocence, beautiful and comely in full light, satisfying but never tiring. Great peace is with You, as is untroubled life.* — *Confessions 2, 10*

NOVEMBER 26
Love Eternal Life

L ET us love eternal life. Let us learn how much we ought to strive for eternal life from the way in which those who love the present life labor so much to preserve it.

So much labor, so much striving, so much expense, so much importance, so much attention, and so much care are expended that someone may live a bit longer. What then ought to be done so that such a one may live forever!

— *Sermon 127, 2*

PRAYER. *Lord, I will not quit until You gather all the fragments of myself from my present scatteredness and deformity, and unite them and cement them for eternity into the peace of our dear homeland, my God, my Mercy.*

— *Confessions 12, 16*

NOVEMBER 27

The Eternal Jerusalem "on High"

CLEARLY, the Jerusalem "on high" is also eternal, but the one that existed on earth was only a shadow of the other. The earthly one lasted during the time when the Messiah was announced; the other one enjoys the eternity of our restoration.

During this life, we are exiles from this Jerusalem on high. — *Commentary on Psalm 125, 1*

PRAYER. *Lord, let me journey on my way remembering Jerusalem and raising my heart to her: Jerusalem my Home, Jerusalem my Mother. In that city, the first fruits of my spirit already dwell, and from this I draw assurance of future safety.* — *Confessions 12, 16*

NOVEMBER 28

Time of Mercy

NOW is the time of mercy, for us to correct ourselves. The time for judgment has not yet come. There is no need to despair.

Because of our human, pardonable, and more trivial sins, God has established in the Church set times for requesting mercy. We have a daily medicine in our saying "Forgive us our debts as we forgive our debtors," so that we may share in the Body and Blood of Christ. — *Sermon 17, 5*

PRAYER. *O Lord, give us Your Christ; let us know and see Him—and rejoice.*

— *Commentary on Psalm 84, 9*

NOVEMBER 29

Live for the Lord's Coming

MY brothers and sisters, believe firmly what you believe—that Christ will return. What does it matter when? Prepare yourself for His coming.

Live as though He were coming today, and you will not fear His coming. *— Sermon 265, 3-4*

PRAYER. Enter not into judgment of me, O Lord, my God! I may imagine myself to be ever so just, but when you bring forth Your treasury and apply it to me, I am found to be evil. Enter not into judgment of Your servant! I am in need of mercy, for I am a fugitive returning and seeking peace. But I am not worthy to be called Your child. *— Commentary on Psalm 142, 6*

NOVEMBER 30

Christ Makes Us Beautiful

OUR every breath yearns for Christ. He alone is the Desired One, the most beautiful of all.

Christ loved us in our unloveliness, in order to make us beautiful like Himself.

— Sermon on John 10, 13

PRAYER. Lord, I want to see Your face. I will persevere in this search, since I am not seeking to see something base but rather Your face, my Lord. May I thus love You freely, since I have found nothing more precious than You.

— Commentary on Psalm 26 (1), 8

DECEMBER 1

Love Will Sing

UNDENIABLY, in heaven we shall see, we shall love, and we shall praise. Our vision will never fail, our love will never end, and our praise will never fall silent.

Love sings now; then, too, it is love that will sing. But now it is a yearning love that sings; then it will be an enjoying love.　*— Sermon 254, 6*

PRAYER.　*O Lord, my God, You alone do I love. You alone do I follow. You alone do I seek. You alone am I prepared to serve, for You alone justly rule, and under Your authority I long to be.*

— Soliloquies 1, 1

DECEMBER 2

Let Us Wake Up!

LIFT up your heart so that it will not rot on earth. This is the advice given by Him Who wishes not to destroy but to save. You will not lose what You have given Him, but you will follow it to heaven.

You will not remain without treasure, but you will possess without worries in heaven what you have to guard here in fear. And so let us wake up.

— Sermon 60, 7

PRAYER.　*O Lord, I ask You for instruction, that through my trials I may learn what I should seek. I ask You, then, for eternal life. Please hear me: it is a place at Your right hand I seek.*

— Commentary on Psalm 59, 1

DECEMBER 3

The Final Rest

NCE we are in heaven, we shall be at rest and we shall see. We shall see and we shall love. We shall love and we shall praise.

The end of our desires will be the One Who can be admired without end, can be loved without our being bored, and can be praised without our becoming tired. — *City of God 22, 30*

PRAYER. *You have made us for Yourself, O Lord, and our hearts are restless until they rest in You.* — *Confessions 1, 1*

DECEMBER 4

The Right Choice

NOWING that the last day is coming is useful to us, and not knowing when it is coming is just as useful. Thus, we may have no fear of that day, but even love it. For that day increases the task of unbelievers but ends the task of believers.

It is now in your power to choose which of these possibilities you desire, before that day arrives. But once it has arrived, this possibility will no longer exist. So make your choice now, while you have time, because God mercifully delays what He conceals. — *Commentary on Psalm 36, 1*

PRAYER. *O happy home! O land of safety! May I dwell there in security! From there I shall not seek to depart, for no safer place shall I find.*
— *Sermon 217, 2*

DECEMBER 5
Our Desire Is Before God

ALL my desire is before You, O Lord. For our desire is not before human beings, who cannot read our heart.

Therefore, let your desire be always before God; and your Father Who sees in secret will repay you. For your constant desire is your prayer; and if your desire is constant, so is your prayer constant. — *Commentary on psalm 37, 14*

PRAYER. *Lord, whatever You give me is too little for me. Be Yourself my inheritance! I love You without reserve: with all my heart and all my soul and all my mind. Of what value is anything You give me that is not Yourself!*

— *Sermon 334, 3*

DECEMBER 6
Woe to Those Guided by Pride

NOW woe to those who are guided by pride, for they will necessarily fall. We see human works. Mercy feeds the poor; so does pride. In the external works themselves we see no distinction.

But enter into your conscience and examine it. If your heart does not accuse you that you act out of vainglory, it is well to be without fear. Fear only to act for the purpose of being praised.

— *Sermon on 1 John 8, 9*

PRAYER. *O Lord, hear me and turn Your face to me. See me and pity me and heal me. In Your eyes I have become an enigma to myself, and that is my infirmity.* — *Confessions 10, 33*

DECEMBER 7
St. Ambrose, Servant of God

REACHING Milan, I found your devoted servant Ambrose, who was known throughout the world as a man whom there were few to equal in goodness.

Unknown to me, it was You Who led me to him, so that I might knowingly be led by him to You. — *Confessions 5, 13*

PRAYER. Let me now seek You, O Lord, calling upon You. And let me call upon You, believing in You, for You have been preached to us. My faith calls upon You—a faith that You have inspired in me by the Incarnation of Your Son through the ministry of Your preacher. — Confessions 1, 1

DECEMBER 8
Mary, the Mother

O manifest infirmity, O wondrous humility, in which all the greatness of God lay hidden! The mother to whom His infancy was subject, He ruled with His power; and to her at whose breasts He nursed, He gave the nourishment of truth.

May He Who did not shrink from making a beginning like ours, perfect in us His gifts. And may He also make us children of God, He Who for our sakes wished to become a human child.

— *Sermon 184, 3*

PRAYER. Let our beautiful God, the Word with God, come to us that we may gaze upon Him with the eyes of our minds.

— *Commentary on Psalm 44, 3*

DECEMBER 9
Invite the Lord into Your Hearts

EE, the voice cries out in the desert; it breaks the silence. "Make straight," it cries out, "the way of the Lord." In other words, I vibrate in your ears only to let the Lord enter into your hearts.

But He will enter where I am to introduce Him only if your ardent prayer invites Him.

— Sermon 293, 4

PRAYER. *O my soul, why are you so distracted by things? Why are you so occupied with earthly and mortal cares? Stay with me and praise the Lord!* *— Commentary on Psalm 145, 6*

DECEMBER 10
The Coming of Christ

HE only Son of God was to come to earth, to become a man, and in this nature to be born as man. He was to die, to rise again, to ascend to heaven, to sit at the right hand of the Father, and to fulfill His promises among the nations.

After that He was to come again to execute His threats against the wicked and to reward the just as He had promised. *— Commentary on Psalm 110, 3*

PRAYER. *Lord, we are Your little flock; we belong to You. Spread Your wings that we may take refuge under them. Be our glory, let us be loved for Your sake, and let Your word be feared in our midst.* *— Confessions 10, 36*

DECEMBER 11

Promises of God Fulfilled in Christ

BECAUSE God's promises seemed impossible to human beings—equality with the angels in exchange for mortality, corruption, poverty, weakness, dust, and ashes—God established a mediator of His good faith: not a prince or angel, but His only Son.

God wanted, through His Son, to show and give us the way He would lead us to the goal He has promised. — *Commentary on Psalm 110, 3*

PRAYER. *Good Father, You loved us so much that You did not spare Your only Son, but handed Him over for the sake of us sinners. How great was Your love for us!* — *Confessions 10, 43*

DECEMBER 12

Count on the Lord's Help

WHEN Peter counted on the Lord's help, it enabled him to walk on the water. When human frailty made him falter he turned once more to the Lord.

Jesus immediately stretched out His hand to help him, raised him up as he was sinking, and rebuked him for his lack of faith. — *Sermon 76, 8*

PRAYER. *I pray to You, my God, for to turn from You is to fall; to turn to You is to rise again; to remain in You is to stand firm. Come to me in Your mercy.* — *Soliloquies 1, 3*

DECEMBER 13

Contemplation and Activity

 ONE of us should be so given to contemplation that in this condition we give no thought to our neighbor's needs; not so given to activity that we allow no time for the contemplation of God.

Therefore, the love of truth seeks out holy leisure, while the compelling force of love takes on necessary activity. Nonetheless, the delight for learning should never be entirely abandoned.

— *City of God 19, 19*

PRAYER. *O God, come to me in Your kindness. For You are the good and the beautiful in Whom, by Whom, and through Whom all things are good and beautiful.* — *Soliloquies 1, 1*

DECEMBER 14

St. John the Baptist

 ANY things could be said about St. John the Baptist. However, If I attempted to enumerate them, I would never be finished with telling you, nor you with listening.

Now let me round if off in a nutshell. Human beings must be humbled, and God must be exalted. — *Sermon 293 D, 5*

PRAYER. *This is my glory, Lord my God, that I might proclaim to You forever that there is nothing from myself for me. All good things come from You, for You are God, all things in all.*

— *Commentary on Psalm 29, 13*

DECEMBER 15

Christ Is the Way and the Haven

IRECTLY through the man Christ you go to the God Christ. The Word that was far from you became man in your midst.

Where you are to abide, He is God; on your way there, He is man. Christ Himself is both the Way by which you go and the Haven toward which you make your way. — *Sermon 261, 7*

PRAYER. *Let those laboring under a burden listen to You, kind Jesus. Let them not presume to lift their eyes to heaven, just as the sinner in the Gospel beat his breast and approached only from a distance.* — *Holy Virginity 36, 36*

DECEMBER 16

Clean Faces

AVE we sinned? Let us correct ourselves! The way has not yet ended; the day is not over. For human and tolerable sins, God has established in the Church a time of mercy for distributing a daily medicine.

It occurs at Mass when we say: "Forgive us our trespasses . . . ." By these words, therefore, with a face washed clean we approach the table to receive Christ's Body and Blood — *Sermon 17, 5*

PRAYER. *May Christ perfect His gifts in us, since He did not hesitate to take our faults on Himself. And may He make us children of God, since for our sakes He chose to become the Son of human beings.* — *Sermon 184, 3*

DECEMBER 17

Born of a Woman

JUST imagine the incredible kindness and mercy! He was the only Son, but He did not want to remain alone. So that humans might be born of God, God was born of humans.

Begotten of God is He through Whom, we were created; born of a woman is He through Whom we are to be re-created. The Word first wished to be born of humans, so that you might be assured of being born of God. — *Sermon on John 2, 13*

PRAYER. *O Word before all time, by Whom time was made, born in time although You are eternal life, You call us who are bound by time and make us eternal.* — *Commentary on Psalm 101 (2), 10*

DECEMBER 18

Christ Our Mediator

CHRIST is the spouse, the mediator between God and humanity—this inasmuch as He is man. For inasmuch as He is God, He is no mediator but is equal to the Father. How ever could we come to God when such distances had to be traversed?

God Himself remains God; humanity is assumed by God. There results a single person. Here is God, our liberator; here is man, our mediator. — *Sermon 293, 7*

PRAYER. *Lord, within the bulwark of Your love and mercy, protect me.*

— *Commentary on Psalm 16, 8*

DECEMBER 19
Toward the Father

SSENTIALLY, what is the way through which we run? Christ said: "I am the Way." What is the homeland to which we are running? Christ said: "I am the Truth." You run through Him, you run to Him, and you rest in Him.

We were sick and could not move. And so the Physician came to the patient; the way was prepared for the wanderers. Let us be saved by Him; let us walk through Him. — *Sermon on 1 John 10, 1*

PRAYER. *Lord, my God, listen to my prayer, and may Your mercy hear my desire.*

— *Confessions 11, 2*

DECEMBER 20
The Way Comes to You

UR Lord said: "I am the Way, I am the Truth, I am the Life." The Truth, all the while remaining with the Father, became the Way also when He assumed our flesh.

No one says to you: "Labor and find the Way" so that you may come to the Truth and the Life. Get up, lazy one! The Way Himself has come to you and roused you from slumber.

— *Sermon 142, 1*

PRAYER. *How great was Your love for us, kind Father! You did not spare Your sole-begotten Son but surrendered Him for the sake of us sinners!* — *Confessions 10, 43*

185

DECEMBER 21
Time of Healing

RECALL that the human race lay sick, because of its sins.

To heal this great body of the sick the Almighty Physician came down from heaven. He humbled Himself to take mortal flesh to Himself, coming to the sick bed.

Come to this Physician. This is the time to be healed, not the time for vain pleasure.

— Sermon 87, 13

PRAYER. *Lord, You are my helper and the helper of everyone who reaches out to You. Indeed, You are my Redeemer for the very purpose of enabling me to reach out to You.*

— Commentary on Psalm 18, 15

DECEMBER 22
Humility Does the Will of God

MERE human being that you are, why are you proud? God became humble for your sake! Perhaps you would be ashamed to imitate a humble man; then at least imitate a humble God. The Son of God came as a man and became humble.

Your whole humility consists in knowing yourself. Pride does its own will; humility does the will of God. *— Sermon on John 25, 16*

PRAYER. *You come, O Christ, humble in appearance! Filled with Your love, your followers preached in praise of Your humility throughout the world of the nations.*

— Commentary on Psalm 53, 4

DECEMBER 23

You Can Now Reach Out

GOD became a man for this purpose: since you, a human being, could not reach God, but you can reach other humans, you might now reach God through a man. And so the man Christ Jesus became the mediator of God and human beings.

God became a man so that following a man—something you are able to do—you might reach God, which was formerly impossible to you.

— *Commentary on Psalm 134, 5*

PRAYER. *Lord, You are delightful food for the pure of heart.* — *Confessions 13, 21*

DECEMBER 24

Humble yet Extraordinary

ASSUREDLY, Christ's human birth was both humble and extraordinary. Why humble? Because as man He was born of a human creature. Why extraordinary? Because He was born of a virgin.

Virgin she conceived, virgin she gave birth, virgin she remained! — *The Creed 3, 6*

PRAYER. *Come, let us adore Him Whom the Virgin conceived without concupiscence, to Whom she gave birth as a virgin and remained thereafter a virgin.* — *Sermon 231, 2*

DECEMBER 25

It is Christ's Birthday

REJOICE you who are just. It is the birthday of Him Who justifies. Rejoice you who are weak and sick. It is the birthday of Him Who makes people well. Rejoice you who are in captivity. It is the birthday of the Redeemer. Rejoice you who are slaves. It is the birthday of the Master.

Rejoice you who are free. It is the birthday of Him Who makes us free. Rejoice all you Christians. It is Christ's birthday. — *Sermon 184, 2*

PRAYER. *Let us devoutly celebrate this day, For just as the first ones to share our faith adored Christ lying in the manger, let us adore Him reigning in heaven.* — *Sermon 203, 3*

DECEMBER 26

God Became Man

AWAKE, mankind! For your sake God has become man. Awake, you who sleep, and rise from the dead, and Christ will enlighten you.

I tell you again, for your sake Christ has become man. If He had not been born in time, you would have been dead for all eternity.

— *Sermon 185, 1*

PRAYER. *Rise up, Lord, help us, and redeem us because of Your Name.*

— *Commentary on Psalm 43, 26*

DECEMBER 27

Love One Another after Christ's Example

NQUESTIONABLY, the Lord marked out for us the fullness of love we ought to have for one another when He told us: "There is no greater love than to lay down one's life for one's friend."

The evangelist John, in his first letter, tells us that we ought to lay down our lives for others in the same way as Christ laid down His life for us. We ought to love one another after the example of Christ. *— Sermon on John 84, 1*

PRAYER. *Lord, You are my helper that I may dwell in Your love, my redeemer that You may deliver me from my wrongdoing.*

— Commentary on Psalm 18 (2), 16

DECEMBER 28

Take Advantage of Little Things

EE, we are heading toward great things. Let us take advantage of the little things and we will become great. Do you want to reach the heights of God? Take hold first of the humility of God.

Put on the humility God. Put on the humility of Christ. Learn to be humble; do not grow proud.

— Sermon 117, 17

PRAYER. *Alas for me, O Lord, how high You are in the heights, and how deep in the depths! Nowhere do You withdraw, yet we scarcely return to You!* *— Confessions 8, 3*

DECEMBER 29

A Great Event

OW the Lord established a civilization into which to be born, just as He created a mother from whom to be born. These events we have all celebrated in song.

This He has done Who raises up the poor to place them in the company of princes. This is a great event, a great joy!

— *Commentary on Psalm 86, 7-8*

PRAYER. *Let Christ help you, the Son of the Virgin and the spouse of virgins, physically born of the virginal womb and spiritually joined in virginal marriage!* — *Holy Virginity 2, 2*

DECEMBER 30

Mary and the Word

ARY, whence does this great good happen to you? You are a virgin, you are holy, and you have made a vow. Whence does this happen to you? He Who made you is formed in you.

Yes, He by Whom heaven and earth were made, by Whom all things were made, He the Word of God, takes flesh in you and assumes it without losing His divinity. — *Sermon 291, 6*

PRAYER. *Let our beautiful God, the Word with God, come to us that we may gaze upon Him with the eyes of our minds. He was beautiful in the womb of the Virgin where, in taking on our humanity, He nonetheless did not lose His divinity.* — *Commentary on Psalm 44, 3*

DECEMBER 31

Son of Mary

 HRIST was born in a unique way of God without a mother, from a human mother without a father. He was born in the last period of time. He came through a woman, His mother, the Lord of heaven and earth. He is certainly the Lord of Mary also.

As the creator of heaven and earth, He is the creator of Mary. But according to the statement of St. Paul, "born of a woman," He is the Son of Mary. The same Lord of Mary is the Son of Mary. The very creator of Mary was born of Mary!

— *Sermon on John 8, 8-9*

PRAYER. *Glory to our Lord and to His mercy and to His truth! Out of His mercy He did not fail to make us blessed, not did He hide from us His truth. The Truth, clad in flesh, came to us and healed through His flesh the inner eye of our heart, that afterward we might be able to see Him face to face.* — *Commentary on Psalm 56, 17*

Augustine's Great Canticle of Love

MY love of You, God, is not some vague
feeling;
it is positive and certain.
Your word struck into my heart
and from that moment I loved You.
Besides this, all about me,
heaven and earth and all that they contain
proclaim that I should love You.

But what do I love when I love You?
Not material beauty of a temporal order;
not the brilliance of earthly light;
not the sweet melody of harmony and song;
not the fragrance of flowers, perfumes, and
spices;
not manna or honey;
and not limbs the body delights to embrace.

It is not these that I love when I love my God.
And yet, when I love Him,
it is true that I love a light of a certain kind,
a voice, a perfume, a food, an embrace;
but they are the kind that I love in my inner
self,
when my soul is bathed in light that is not
bound by space;
when it listens to sound that never dies away;
when it breathes fragrance that is not borne
away on the wind;
when it tastes food that is never consumed
by the eating;
when it clings to an embrace from which
it is not severed by fulfillment of desire.
This is what I love when I love my God.

Confessions 10, 6-8

192

OTHER OUTSTANDING CATHOLIC BOOKS